THE EPISTLES OF JOHN

NCCS | New Covenant Commentary Series

The New Covenant Commentary Series (NCCS) is designed for ministers and students who require a commentary that interacts with the text and context of each New Testament book and pays specific attention to the impact of the text upon the faith and praxis of contemporary faith communities.

The NCCS has a number of distinguishing features. First, the contributors come from a diverse array of backgrounds in regards to their Christian denominations and countries of origin. Unlike many commentary series that tout themselves as international the NCCS can truly boast of a genuinely international cast of contributors with authors drawn from every continent of the world (except Antarctica) including countries such as the United States, Puerto Rico, Australia, the United Kingdom, Kenya, India, Singapore, and Korea. We intend the NCCS to engage in the task of biblical interpretation and theological reflection from the perspective of the global church. Second, the volumes in this series are not verse-by-verse commentaries, but they focus on larger units of text in order to explicate and interpret the story in the text as opposed to some often atomistic approaches. Third, a further aim of these volumes is to provide an occasion for authors to reflect on how the New Testament impacts the life, faith, ministry, and witness of the New Covenant Community today. This occurs periodically under the heading of "Fusing the Horizons and Forming the Community." Here authors provide windows into community formation (how the text shapes the mission and character of the believing community) and ministerial formation (how the text shapes the ministry of Christian leaders).

It is our hope that these volumes will represent serious engagements with the New Testament writings, done in the context of faith, in service of the church, and for the glorification of God.

Series Editors:
Michael F. Bird (Ridley College, Melbourne, Australia)
Craig Keener (Asbury Theological Seminary, Wilmore, KY, USA)

Titles in this series:
Romans Craig Keener
Ephesians Lynn Cohick
Colossians and Philemon Michael F. Bird
Revelation Gordon Fee
John Jey Kanagaraj
1 Timothy Aída Besançon Spencer
2 Timothy and Titus Aída Besançon Spencer
Mark Kim Huat Tan
2 Peter and Jude Andrew Mbuvi
1–2 Thessalonians Nijay Gupta
1 Corinthians B. J. Oropeza
Luke Diane G. Chen

Forthcoming titles:
James Pablo Jimenez
Matthew Jason Hood
1 Peter Sean du Toit
Philippians Linda Belleville
Hebrews Cynthia Westfall
Galatians Jarvis Williams
2 Corinthians Ayodeji Adewuya

THE EPISTLES OF JOHN

Their Message and Relevance for Today

A New Covenant Commentary

Samuel M. Ngewa

▲ CASCADE *Books* • Eugene, Oregon

THE EPISTLES OF JOHN
Their Message and Relevance for Today

New Covenant Commentary

Copyright © 2019 Samuel M. Ngewa. All rights reserved. Except for brief quotations in critical publications or reviews, no part of this book may be reproduced in any manner without prior written permission from the publisher. Write: Permissions, Wipf and Stock Publishers, 199 W. 8th Ave., Suite 3, Eugene, OR 97401.

A New Covenant Commentary

Cascade Books
An Imprint of Wipf and Stock Publishers
199 W. 8th Ave., Suite 3
Eugene, OR 97401

www.wipfandstock.com

PAPERBACK ISBN: 978-1-60899-862-3
HARDCOVER ISBN: 978-1-4982-8751-7
EBOOK ISBN: 978-1-4982-4118-2

Cataloguing-in-Publication data:

Names: Ngewa, Samuel M., author.

Title: The epistles of John : their message and relevance for today : a new covenant commentary / Samuel M. Ngewa.

Description: Eugene, OR: Cascade Books, 2019 | Series: New Covenant Commentary | Includes bibliographical references and index.

Identifiers: ISBN 978-1-60899-862-3 (paperback) | ISBN 978-1-4982-8751-7 (hardcover) | ISBN 978-1-4982-4118-2 (ebook)

Subjects: LCSH: Bible. Epistles of John—Commentaries.

Classification: BS2805.3 2019 (print) | BS2805.3 (ebook)

Manufactured in the U.S.A.   OCTOBER 11, 2019

*Dedicated to all the preachers, teachers, and students
of the word of God,
whose genuine desire is to pass on true doctrine and purity of life,
both to their generation and others to come*

Contents

Outline | *ix*
Preface | *xi*
About This Commentary | *xiii*
Abbreviations | *xv*

Introduction | 1
1 John | 9
2 John | 98
3 John | 111
Summary and Conclusion | 129

    Fusing Horizons | 130

Appendix | *137*
Bibliography | *141*
Scripture Index | *145*
Author Index | *149*
Subject Index | *151*
Greek Concepts Index | *152*

Outline

Some Matters of Introduction
    Authorship
    Date and Place of Writing
    The Historical Context
    Form/Genre and Purpose

First Epistle of John
    Reliable Testimony and Its Goal (1:1–4)
    Inescapable Fact and Its Implication (1:5–10)
    The Intended Goal—Not to Sin (2:1–6)
    The Ageless Commandment—Old Yet New (2:7–17)
        Love Toward a Brother or Sister
        Love Toward the Father
    The Present Enemy (2:18–27)
    Our Status and Obligation as Children of God (2:28—3:10)
    Love, a Distinctive Characteristic of a Believer (3:11–18)
        The Commandment of Love
        Examples of Love—Negative and Positive
        The Practice of Love
    The Wonderful Confidence (3:19–24)
    The Clear Demarcation (4:1–6)
    The Triangle of Love (4:7–21)
        Vertical Love
        Response Love
        Horizontal Love
        Mystery of This Love
        Summary
    The Final Test (5:1–5)
    The Undisputable Evidence (5:6–12)

Outline

The Ultimate Reward—Eternal Life (5:13–21)

Second Epistle of John
    Translation
    Commentary

Third Epistle of John
    Translation
    Commentary
        Gaius (vv. 1–8)
        Diotrephes (vv. 9–11)
        Demetrius (v. 12)
        Concluding Remarks and Greetings (vv. 13–15)

Summary and Conclusion

Preface

On September 1, 2017, the Chief Justice of the Republic of Kenya, David Maraga, prefaced the decision of the Supreme Court of which he chaired with the words, "The greatness of any nation lies in its fidelity to the constitution and adherence to the rule of law and above all the fear of God."[1] He then went on to tell the nation (Kenya), and the world, that the presidential election held in Kenya on August 8, 2017, was not conducted according to the rules and so was to be repeated. Nullification of elections at that level is rare,[2] but for Chief Justice Maraga and the majority of his team of judges, their action was justified because the set standards must be met.

There is a kingdom above all nations of the earth, and the ruler of that kingdom is God himself. It is he who created all things and all rulers of nations govern on his behalf. He sets different ones on the throne and removes them as he wills. Those who belong to this kingdom are called believers because they have certain truths that they believe in, with the highest truth being that God has sent a Savior into the world whose name is Jesus Christ. Members of this kingdom are also called children of God, and as such they have God-given standards they must live by. Today, they are located all over the world but this is the outcome of what began in Jerusalem, on the day

---

1. The writer of this work witnessed the reading of the judgment personally, and the same was carried by the newspapers the following day. The same court gave a full verdict on the matter on September 20, 2017. While the majority of judges focused on the ethics of the election (arguing that it matters how one gets the numbers), the minority focused on the numbers that had been announced earlier. The center of disagreement was whether quality takes preeminence over quantity or not. The Epistles of John raise the same question, with a clear answer. Hopefully this work will bring some of this out, as a general principle for Christian living.

2. Nullification of a presidential election had never happened in Africa before this, and in the world only a few countries, like Maldives and Austria, had done it (Peter Kagwanja, *Kenyan Sunday Nation*, September 1, 2017, 29).

of Pentecost, and then spread outwardly until the ends of the earth were reached, and are still being reached. Their constitution is the Bible.

The Epistles of John were written to such members of the kingdom of God, most likely located at Ephesus or its vicinity in Asia Minor. The message of the first letter centers on the need to live a life that reflects God's nature as light and love, and to firmly hold on to the truth that Jesus is the Christ come in the flesh. The second letter also lays emphasis on the exercise of love and correct belief as to who Jesus is. The focus of the third letter is hospitality, especially to those traversing regions to proclaim the good news of salvation in Christ. Whether addressing matters of belief or practice, the central issue is: What is it that should characterize children of God? Relating this to the words of Maraga quoted above, but now applying to the kingdom of kingdoms, we can say, "The maturity of a believer lies in the soundness of his or her beliefs and the sincerity of his or her practice." This is what John seeks to advance in the lives of his readers. The same test applies to us also, no matter our social status, as we live in our corners of the world in the twenty-first century.

In this commentary, therefore, the meaning of the biblical text will not be an end to itself. Every effort will be made to move from exegesis to application, as may be necessary. This, however, will be done in a general manner because the needs of the different locations where God's children live in are varied. In any case, the overall point of application is that we who are believers must rise up to the occasion and face all the challenges of our day as we relate to our God who is light, relate to other believers who are our spiritual brothers and sisters, reach out to bring others (unbelievers) to the wonderful fellowship in the family of God, and remain true to the teachings of Jesus to us, through the apostles.

About This Commentary

This commentary is written with the acknowledgement that it only amounts to, say, a bucket of water from Lake Victoria. Many other commentaries have been, are being, and will be written on the same books of the Bible traditionally referred to as the Epistles of John. Writing commentaries is more or less like the preaching that goes on all the time; only that it takes longer time and is more costly. Just as we may have a preacher doing a series on a book of the Bible to a congregation in London and another one doing the same to a congregation in Lagos (these cities selected for no special reason), so also are commentaries. The message of the Bible is so rich and important that the more it is passed on the better, and the more the persons who pass it on the better still. Each of us, however, passes it on within the limitations of our accent[1] and understanding. I am grateful to brothers and Drs. Michael Bird and Craig S. Keener (extensively published scholars) who have organized some of us to write the New Covenant Commentary Series so that our "accents" can also be part of the millions of them from other regions of the world.

Those of us who are privileged to make a contribution by way of pen (now replaced by the laptop) and finger (in comparison to preachers who use the pulpit and tongue) do also bring our own personalities, experiences, and life goals. For me, for example, I have noticed that I am more concerned about a statement of review of my writing by a pastor in Accra (used for no special reason) how I related the message of Scripture to the African context than a statement of review on how I failed to explore this or the other theory in my commenting, so long as what I have said correctly

---

1. In his book, *Healers to Physicians*, Japheth K. G. Mati (a renown Kenyan medical professor and researcher) tells of an experience in Gainesville, Florida, where a waitress instructed another "take tea to that guy with an accent" (referring to him) and then Mati adds, "Actually I thought she was the one speaking with an accent" (172). Needless to say, our worldview is an accent in itself, and we all have one.

About This Commentary

represents my understanding of the author's message. In the budgeting of time I spent in doing this work, I was more focused on what within my limitations I understand John (as will be shown below, John the apostle is assumed to be the author) to have meant when he wrote to his readers and how that applies to us today. What others say John meant is acknowledged, especially in footnotes, but without taking time to argue extensively with them. In my attempt to make clear why I understood a statement this or that way, I have in some places used the concept of shades or aspect of Greek verb tenses and noun cases. Definitions and some explanation of all the ones that are used in the work are provided as an appendix. The translation provided in the work is my own translation from the United Bible Societies Greek New Testament. Comments on variations in the readings from different manuscripts are kept to a minimum. Greek words are used in transliterated form except in a few places where they are a title of work used in this commentary. It is easier for a Greek student to convert the transliterated form into Greek than for a non-Greek student to use the work if Greek letters are used.

It is my hope and prayer that many students of Scripture will find this work a beneficial tool to work and interact with as they seek to understand God's message to us and apply it in our times.

For words that have come to have two acceptable spellings, like savior and saviour, honor and honour, etc., the shorter spelling has been used, but without any prejudice. Also, small letters are used for pronouns (he, his, him, etc.) which stand for God, Jesus, and Holy Spirit but with full reverence and worship. They are used solely for simplicity in expression.

Abbreviations

1QS	*Serek Hayyahad*, Community Rule (Manual of Discipline) from Qumran Cave 1
DNTT	Dictionary of New Testament Theology
DNA	Deoxyribonucleic Acid
Eccl. Hist.	Ecclesiastical History
HCSB	Holman Christian Standard Bible
NASB	New American Standard Bible
NIV	New International Version
NKJB	New King James Bible
NRSV	New Revised Standard Version
TDNT	Theological Dictionary of the New Testament
TNIV	Today's New International Version
UBS	United Bible Societies

Introduction

The focus of this work is not issues of introduction but the teaching of the three letters. However, for their teaching to be explored fairly, an author has to work with certain conclusions, whether by way of assumption or well-argued discussion. The brief discussion below spells out the matters of authorship, date and place of writing, the historical context, and the question of genre or form and purpose.

AUTHORSHIP

Unlike the Pastoral epistles (and some other epistles in the New Testament) whose Pauline authorship is questioned by many, and I have maintained in my writings that we cannot deny the truthfulness of the books' claim that Paul wrote them (1 Tim 1:1; 2 Tim 1:1; and Titus 1:1) without diluting the authority of the rest of the books' content,[1] the three books traditionally called Epistles of John do not make mention of John at all.[2] The first epistle goes directly to the message without a mention of who the author or the recipient are.[3] The second and third epistles do better because they mention

---

1. Ngewa 2009: 1.

2. The three epistles, and especially 1 John, resemble the book of Hebrews in this respect, about which a failure to accept the once held view that Paul wrote it is the more common trend even among those who prefer maintaining the traditional positions on these matters. Almost everyone uses "the author of Hebrews" over against saying "Paul" or someone else by name when making reference to the content of Hebrews.

3. A mention of the recipient is totally lacking, and the use of the first person plural (we) in the opening verses does not help much, except to tell us that the author was an eyewitness to the earthly life and ministry of Christ. The common practice in the first century was for a writer to begin by specifying who is writing and who the recipient is (in the New Testament, Pauline epistles adopt these features extensively), among other features like good wish or prayer (Doty 1973: 14). This has even led to discussions of

that the author is "the elder" (*ho presbyteros*) but without a name (2 John 1 and 3 John 1). Nevertheless I will, in this work, assume John the apostle to be the author. Apart from the defense of this traditional view in many books on New Testament introduction and other commentaries,[4] there is a general view in the African context that when it comes to matters of history, information from the elders is more dependable than statements of later generations, unless good reason is provided for why the elders may have told lies.[5]

The traditional position on the authorship of 1 John is tied to the authorship of the Gospel of John, and the authorship of the Gospel of John is tied to the identity of the disciple of John 21:24 who is described in 21:20 as "the disciple whom Jesus loved." By implication, therefore, the internal evidence concerning the author is dependent on points that require to be argued out. The relationship between the Gospel and 1 John is primarily seen in the use of common language,[6] and the identity of the disciple of John 21:24 is based on an argument of elimination of any other disciple until we are left with John the son of Zebedee.[7]

---

whether the three books commented on in this work should be referred to as epistles or even letters. From the bibliography at the end of this work, it is noticeable that less and less authors are using "epistles" or "letters" in the title of their works on the three books. This, however, is a secondary issue to the message of the books. It is very clear that behind the message was an author and the message is directed to specific readers (see discussion on genre/form below).

4. See, among others, Guthrie 1970: 864–69; and Painter 2003: 44–51.

5. The argument that it was not uncommon to have a document attached to an authoritative figure for the purpose of its acceptance has been proposed, to explain away the traditional view, but that needs to be weighed against the extent of testimony of the early church fathers.

6. A significant point of similarity between the Gospel of John and 1 John is the use of vocabularies such as *logos* (word) found in John 1:1, 14 and 1 John 1:1 to refer to Jesus, *paraklētos* (advocate/comforter) in John 14:16, 26; 15:26; 16:7; and 1 John 2:1; *entolē kainē* (new commandment) in John 13:34 and 1 John 2:7, 8; and *gennaō* (I give birth to) in John 3:3, 4, 5, 6, 7, 8; and 1 John 2:29; 3:9; 4:7; 5:1, 4, 18, just to mention some. For more detailed listing, see Brooke 1912: i–xix; Painter 2003: 58–73; and Jobes 2014: 25–27. The use of dualism (for example darkness and light, love and hate, truth and falsehood, God and devil) is also another important element of similarity between the two writings.

7. Assumption is usually made from a study of the Synoptic Gospels that Peter, James, and John would be the most likely candidates for the description, "disciple whom Jesus loved." While Jesus had twelve disciples, these three constituted what appears to be an inner circle (see, time of transfiguration: Matt 17:1–8; Mark 9:2–19; Luke 9:28–36; occasion of healing Jairus' daughter: Mark 5:37–42; Luke 8:51–56; and at Gethsemane:

Introduction

This internal evidence, though by deduction and not directly stated, is accompanied by statements by the early church fathers. These fathers include Polycarp,[8] Papias,[9] Irenaeus,[10] and others.[11] The closeness to first century dates of these witnesses (for example, Polycarp AD 110 and Papias AD 125) and listing in Muratorian Canon (AD 200) among other factors place the Gospel of John and 1 John early enough for the assumption that John wrote them to be a viable option. It cannot be dismissed without better evidence than what we have at the moment.[12]

Matt 26:37-46; Mark 14:33-42). Peter is eliminated because he is mentioned alongside the disciple whom Jesus loved (John 13:23-24; 20:2; and 21:20-21) and James is eliminated because he was killed no later than AD 44 when Herod Agrippa (the killer) died (Acts 12:2) and no New Testament book was written that early. This leaves John who also meets the criteria of the author having been a Jew and a witness of what is recorded in the gospel. For more on this, see Ngewa 2003: 429-30; and Keener 2003: 89-91.

8. Polycarp lived AD 69-155 and in his letter to the Philippians (7:1) uses words that are a clear quotation from 1 John 4:2-3 and 2 John 7 (Jobes 2014: 31). While this may prove more that the Epistles of John were known to Polycarp than that John wrote them, it does at least weaken one of the arguments used to deny Johannine authorship, that is, they were written after John had died. For Polycarp to have quoted it as authority, the gap between when it was written and when he could have quoted it need to be long enough for its authority to have been established.

9. While Papias's witness, quoted by Eusebius (Eccl. Hist. 3.39), is center of the debate as to whether Papias's use of "Lord's disciple" and "elder" have the same person in view or two persons (John the apostle and his follower), the ambiguity is not sufficient basis to dismiss the view that the two refer to the same person, namely John the apostle (see Carson 1991: 69-70). It is within good judgment to view John the apostle as the same person mentioned twice (as an apostle and then as a living witness), with the first mention placing him alongside Andrew, Peter, Philip, Thomas, James, and Matthew (fellow apostles) while the second mention (using the phrase "John the elder") places him alongside Aristion. Also see Keener 2003: 95-98.

10. Of the several places where Irenaeus quotes from 1 John in his work, "Against Heresies," 3.16.5, is a clear witness for he attributes his quote from 1 John 2:18-22 to Saint John.

11. Others include Clement of Alexandria, Origen, and Tertulian (see Guthrie 1970: 864-65). Schnackenburg says, "The tradition of the early church since the time of Irenaeus (d. 202 CE) and Clement of Alexandria (d. ca. 211) ascribes both GJohn and 1 John unequivocally to John the apostle, the son of Zebedee" (1992: 40-41). See also Yarbrough 2008: 5.

12. The argument that has been most influential to those who deny Johannine authorship is the assumption that beliefs go through a process of thesis, antithesis, and then synthesis (as advocated by F. C. Baur in the nineteenth century) with John belonging to the synthesis stage and therefore written later than first century AD. Without going into details (for that will not serve any purpose here) the basis of this argument is that there is no revelation; all beliefs take the process of thought development. Non Johannine

Just as the similarity between the Gospel of John and 1 John implies the same authorship, so also 2 John in relation to 1 John. 2 John addresses the two issues (the matters of Jesus having come in the flesh and the practice of love among believers) at the center of 1 John's teaching. This implies common authorship also. The vocabulary of 3 John (for example, "truth," "children," and "beloved") also moves it toward 2 John, 1 John, and the Gospel of John. The argument would then be something like: Evidence that John wrote the Gospel (elimination of others and witness of church fathers) → Evidence that the author of the Gospel also wrote 1 John (similarity of content among other characteristics) → the writer of 1 John also wrote 2 John (same subject, and even use of "antichrist" in both) → the author of the Gospel, 1 and 2 John, also wrote 3 John (shared vocabulary and similar opening between 2 and 3 John).

It must, however, be mentioned that not everyone finds this convincing. Some have suggested that the similarities can be explained by the Gospel and the epistles sharing a common source, or guarding the same doctrinal interest, rather than one author.[13] The mention of 1 John by the church fathers may also be viewed, by some, as better serving the point that the letter was in circulation early and not necessarily prove that apostle John was the author. Even with these challenges though, there is no better conclusive alternative to the view that John the apostle wrote all the four and that the church fathers were certain of their assertions. It is on the basis of where the weight lies that John will be assumed throughout this work.

DATE AND PLACE OF WRITING

Having adopted the position that John the apostle wrote both the Gospel of John and 1 John (and by extension 2 and 3 John also) the next question is, "Which of the two was written first, and what is the date for 1 John, and by implication also 2 and 3 John?" This question cannot be answered without

---

authorship, in this case, then becomes an assumption (John belongs to synthesis stage) based on another assumption (there is no revelation, but only development of beliefs). That is not sufficient ground to make us doubt the witness of the church fathers.

13. See for example, deSilva 2004: 452–54. Drawing from the different usage of shared vocabularies and such other observations, deSilva says, "Differences in thought and emphasis, which suggest at least a very different situation, also tend to point to different authors" (2004: 453). Brown also, working with a Johannine community view says, "We have in the Gospel and Epistles traces of development within a particular Christian community over several decades" (1997: 404).

INTRODUCTION

working with some assumptions. A key assumption is that a full story needs to be told before those who deviate from it are rebuked. The Gospel tells the full story so as to show that "Jesus is the Christ, the Son of God" (John 20:31) and in I John those who deny this truth are labelled "antichrist" (1 John 2:22). Working with this assumption, 1 John is to be dated after the date given to the Gospel, or about the same time, but not earlier.[14]

The date needs to be within John's lifetime. Eusebius (Eccl. Hist. 3.23) quotes Irenaeus and Clement of Alexandria as saying that John lived through the reign of Titus Flavius Domitian (emperor of Rome from AD 81 to 96) and into the reign of Trajan (emperor from AD 98 to 117). Given this information and the fact that John wrote in his fairly old age (his use of "children" for the believers implies this) the epistles (also the Gospel of John[15]) need to be dated in the late eighties or early nineties.[16] Regarding from where John wrote, Yarbrough says, "Patristic sources plausibly affirm that in roughly 70–100 John was in Ephesus and ministered there."[17] These details (late eighties or early nineties date, and writing from Ephesus) will be assumed in this commentary.

---

14. Brown also assigns to 1 John a date later than the Gospel but from a different perspective. He works with the assumption of a Johannine School with at least four stages, "the beloved disciple (who was the source of the tradition), the evangelist, the presbyter of the Epistles, and the redactor of the Gospel" (Brown 1988: 106). In the fuller commentary he says, "Most probably I John was written not only after GJohn but after an interval long enough for a debate to have arisen about the implications of GJohn and for a schism to have taken place. Recognizing the approximations, if one dates the evangelist's final work (i.e., GJohn without the redactor's additions) to *ca.* AD 90, I John may feasibly be dated to *ca.* 100" (Brown 1982: 101).

15. See Ngewa 2003: 430. When the alternative position that the writings of John do not all need to be attributed to John but to a Johannine school or community is accepted, the date of one (for example, the Gospel) does not need to be the same time as the other. Those who assume a Johannine community argue that John had disciples who so much took after him that they also thought and expressed themselves like their master. Such scholars see the similarities between the Gospel and the epistles within this context of master-follower influence. The position adopted here, however, is that the similarities exist because the Gospel and the epistles had the same author.

16. Jobes 2014: 29.

17. Yarbrough 2008: 17.

The Historical Context

Within the content of the three epistles, there is in each one of them at least one detail that is helpful in providing a feel of what was happening when John wrote them.

In 1 John 2:19 John talks of those who "have gone out of us." While this will be discussed in more detail in the commentary itself, what this implies is that John's readers are believers whom he had shepherded and they knew his position in matters of essential doctrines and basic Christian living. When he was writing, however, some false teaching had set into the community he had taught the truth and some of the members had been deceived to the point of leaving the congregation of the faithful. Most scholars refer to them as secessionists. Their position on sin seems to be that it did not matter (implied in what John teaches in 1 John 1) and their position on who Jesus is was that he did not come in the flesh, a lie that John refutes to the point of calling those who deny Jesus' humanity the "antichrists" (2:18, 22; 4:3). Their worldview on these matters also seems to have made them downplay the place of love among people of God, against Jesus' teaching that we love one another—a matter to which John gives extensive and repeated attention in the epistle. Lieu suggests that the "us" John uses in 2:19 refers to him and other teachers (for example, the apostles) like him.[18] In other words, the seceding was at the teachers' level and not at the level of members of the congregation. While this is not an impossibility, John seems to be exhorting the entire congregation in a manner (see for example, the use of "if anyone . . ." in chapter 1 and elsewhere in the epistle) that he is establishing them not to follow those who have been led astray. The picture painted does not seem to be just one of potential danger as Lieu proposes, but an existing situation.[19] The assumption that will be adopted in this work is that the "us" of 2:19 refers to John and the faithful ones. He refers to the faithful as "you" from time to time but also, at times, places himself among them and uses "we" or us." The false teachers are referred to as "they" or "them."

In 2 John, we seem to have a faithful congregation that is facing the same issues (attacks) as the readers of 1 John. Promotion of love and defense of truth about Jesus having come in the flesh are also given central

---

18. Lieu 2008: 101.
19. Lieu 2008: 102.

Introduction

place. The only other place (in addition to 1 John) in the New Testament that "antichrist" is used is in this epistle (v. 7).

3 John focuses on hospitality, and from what is said, it is clear that there was one person (Diotrephes) who did not support it as an important practice among believers. It could have been the level of his understanding but it appears to have been more an attitude toward John and the faithful (a matter of the will) than lack of knowledge (a matter of the mind). The addressee (Gaius), however, was keen on hospitality and even exercised it beyond expectation. A third person (Demetrius) seems to have needed the support of Gaius and other faithful ones (or vice versa[20]), and so John recommends him to Gaius in a very positive manner.

Form/Genre and Purpose

A fourth and final matter of introduction we need to make a comment on before we look at the message in these letters has to do with form or genre. This is important because, even as some have commented, it could explain why the same word may be used differently by the same author. Jobes for example says, "Despite some differences that can probably be accounted for by different genre, the letters of John and the gospel of John are closer in language, style, dualistic worldview, and theology than they are to any other NT book."[21]

While the Gospel of John is a deliberate presentation of who Jesus is, the Epistles of John, especially 1 and 2 John, are a defense of that truth. The defense is occasioned by teachings that deviate from the truth expounded in the Gospel. 1 John, by its general nature, may have been addressed to several congregations while 2 and 3 John may have been addressed to particular though different congregations.[22] This, to begin with, could have

---

20. The context is not very clear. Demetrius may have been someone whose company Gaius needs to keep over against Diotrephes who is in the wrong or he could have been someone Gaius needs to lend a helping hand to. In any case, he is a third and important character in 3 John. See fuller discussion in the commentary.

21. Jobes 2014: 27.

22. deSilva (2004: 452), who views the three epistles as written about the same time but to different audiences, relates 1 John to "the most approximate audiences of the author's circle, seeking to insulate them against the secessionists' position and consolidate their allegiance in the wake of the schism"; 2 John to "a more distant house church (or perhaps a set of churches) to warn them about secessionist missionaries, shaping the Christians' perception of those missionaries in advance of their coming to assure their rejection"; and 3 John to "a locale where one church leader has blocked the author's envoy

determined the length of the epistles. While 1 John has five chapters (as we have it divided in what we have now[23]) 2 and 3 John have one chapter each.

The absence of the features of a formal letter or epistle in the first century (for example, author, addressee, greetings, good wish, or prayer) in 1 John and the limited use of the same in 2 and 3 John has led some to prefer viewing them, and especially 1 John, as either a tractate or a kind of manifesto,[24] or a brochure of some kind.[25] The absence of these features not ignored, especially in 1 John, the message definitely has an author (though not named) and recipients. As Culy says, "Recognizing that 1 John represents hortatory discourse is more important than settling the question whether or not it represents an actual letter."[26]

Conclusion

As we approach the text of these three letters, therefore, we will assume that John the apostle wrote the three of them, to different congregations but having some shared problems. He wrote from Ephesus and in the latter years of his life. He wrote the first two letters because the truth (doctrine) and God approved behavior (morality) were under attack. He also wrote the third letter because the exercise of love, in the matter of hospitality specifically, was also under attack. He wrote to exhort the faithful to stand firmly in the true teachings they had received. The twenty-first century church is facing similar challenges and so the message is as relevant to us as it was for John's original readers. It is for this reason that statements of application to our day will be made from time to time. Both "epistles" and "letters" will be used for the three books freely but without implying that they have all the features of a letter or epistle in the first century AD. Nevertheless, they are written with clear purpose of author exhorting recipient(s) on specific matters.

---

from receiving hospitality," seeking to "secure hospitality for the author's missionaries."

23. Chapter and verse divisions are credited to Stephen Langton of the thirteenth century and Robert Estienne of the sixteenth century, respectively (Finegan 1974: 34).

24. Kummel 1975: 437.

25. Smalley 1984: xxxiii.

26. Culy 2004: xiii.

1 JOHN

Unlike most Pauline epistles where we have a clear separation of doctrine (the indicative) from the practice (the imperative), with the latter based on the former, John's structure does not separate the two so neatly. In any case, his exhortation on practical matters does not lack theological foundation. This will become clear as we note how John lays before his readers as bases for their action the nature of God as light and love, with Christ exercising love at the highest level possible. The outline, therefore (see above), is governed more by the content of the different passages of the epistles than some artificial reorganization of the material to come up with an outline that separates doctrine from practice.

RELIABLE TESTIMONY AND ITS GOAL (1:1–4)

> (1:1) What was in existence from the beginning, what we have heard, what we have seen with our eyes, what we beheld and our hands touched, concerning the word of life (2) and the life was revealed, and we have seen and bear witness and announce to you the life which is eternal, which was with the Father and was revealed to us (3) what we have seen and we have heard, we announce to you also, in order that you (yourselves) also may have fellowship with us. And our fellowship is also with the Father and with his Son, Jesus Christ (4) And these (things) we (ourselves[1]) write in order that our[2] joy may have been made complete.

---

[1]. There is a textual variation here, whether the correct reading is second person in dative plural (*humin*, "to you"—see Textus Receptus, represented by the King James Version among English translations) or the first person nominative plural (*hēmeis*, "we" for emphasis—see the UBS Greek New Testament).

[2]. There is also a textual variation here. The Textus Receptus reads *humōn* ("your") while the UBS Greek New Testament reads *hēmōn* ("our").

This passage revolves around the two verbs, "we bear witness" (*martyroumen*) in 1:2 and "we announce" (*apangellomen*), the latter occurring twice in the passage (1:2, 3).

The act of "bearing witness" or "testifying" (*martyrein*) is an important one for John. He uses it thirty-three times in the Gospel,[3] ten times in his epistles,[4] and four times in Revelation.[5] The use of the nouns "witness" or "testimony" (*martyria*) also show the same interest.[6] The idea behind the word, whether in form of a verb or noun, is that of passing on one's experience to others for the purpose of having the readers or hearers stand with the testimony bearer on something that matters. In law courts for example, one who bears witness seeks to convince the judge and others who may be listening that the position the witness bearer takes on the matter is true. The fact that the English word "martyr" comes from it means that what one testifies to be true can also be costly. Within such a context, deep conviction precedes the testifying. This is not to say that there are no false witnesses. Most of those, however, do not bear witness on basis of deep conviction but as an act of pretense. John belabors the point to assert that the witness borne here is true. As Lieu observes, the experience of the "we" gives them the authority to proclaim to the "you" in this epistle.[7]

The act of announcing (*apangellein*) moves that personal experience to the public arena. Stott puts it well when he says that "to bear witness" carries with it "authority of experience" and "to announce" the "authority of commission."[8] As will be pointed out below, John's personal experience (and that of other apostles) is not for private custody but for public utilization. It

---

3. It is found only twice in the Synoptic gospels, Matt 23:31 and Luke 4:22. In the Gospel of John we find it in 1:7, 8, 15, 32, 34; 2:25; 3:11, 26, 28, 32; 4:39, 44; 5:31, 32a, 32b, 33, 36, 37, 39; 7:7; 8:13, 14, 18a, 18b; 10:25; 12:17; 13:21; 15:26, 27; 18:23, 37; 19:35; 21:24.

4. In all of Paul's epistles, it is found no more than eight times. Considering the thirteen Pauline epistles, we find it in Rom 8:21; 10:2; 1 Cor 15:15; 2 Cor 8:3; Gal 4:15; Col 4:13; 1 Tim 5:10; 6:13. The ten times it is found in the Epistles of John are 1 John 1:2; 4:14; 5:6, 7, 9, 10; 3 John 3, 6, 12a, and 12b.

5. It is found in Rev 1:2; 22:16, 18, and 20.

6. The noun is found fourteen times in the Gospel of John (1:7, 19; 3:11, 32, 33; 5:31, 32, 34, 36; 8:13, 14, 17; 19:35; 21:24); seven times in his epistles (1 John 5:9a, 9b, 9c, 10a, 10b; 11; 3 John 12); nine times in Revelation (1:2, 9; 6:9; 11:7; 12:11, 17; 19:10a, 10b; 20:4); and only seven times in the rest of the New Testament (Matt 14:55, 56, 59; Luke 22:71; Acts 22:18; 1 Tim 3:7; Titus 1:13).

7. Lieu 2008: 36.

8. Stott 1964: 61–62.

Reliable Testimony and Its Goal (1:1–4)

is for all to read and enjoy its blessings. In the present context, it bears full authority for public consumption in that it is not only true (shown by his use of different senses in establishing the matter, as will be shown below) but also its bearer has been commissioned.[9] John sees it as the will of God that his readers will know the truth of his message and join the fellowship in which God the Father and the Son are a part of (1:3). John endeavors to accomplish this act of bearing witness and announcing by way of putting into writing what we have in this epistle (1:4). The acts of "bearing witness," "announcing," and "writing" are all expressed using the present tense.[10]

The acts of bearing witness and announcing are expressed using the first person plural "we" also.[11] This could mean that John is including other apostles in the team. If this is so, we need to remember that John is doing so in their absence, as all of the apostles except John had died by this time.[12] John could also be using the editorial "we" so as to avoid a display of "self"

---

9. As said in the introduction, the position taken in this work is that John the apostle is the author of this letter. When Jesus gave what has come to be referred to as "the Great Commission," in Matt 28:19–20, John was part of that audience.

10. Both *martyroumen* (we bear witness) of 1:2 and *apangellomen* (we announce) of 1:2 and 1:3 may be taken as durative present (if seen as a way of life) or iterative present (if seen as the isolated acts of ministry of the word). This is what John and his colleagues have been doing in the past, and John is still doing as he writes to his readers. The shade of *graphomen* (we write) however may best be taken as aoristic. John is thinking of the writing he is now doing in this epistle. The witness abides over the ages; the ministry of proclamation is a standing duty, but our accomplishment can only be one at a time. For John, the task at hand is the writing of this epistle. This is what is in his mind now, though his task now is only a small part of a wider ministry of "bearing witness" and "announcing." As I write this commentary also, I am doing a task which is my own and another brother or sister in Christ may be writing a commentary on the Epistles of John at the same time. All of us, however, are involved in making the word known. Our particular assignments (writing or teaching or preaching etc.) are not in competition but complementary. The field (bearing witness and announcing) is wider than any individual's act of writing can accomplish alone. What is crucial is that our involvement in the tasks we do has the goal of bringing others to the wonderful fellowship with God the Father, God the Son, and other believers (1:3). As John writes, he sees himself in view of "I and all my colleagues" of the past, of the present, and of the future.

11. The present tense verbs (see previous note above) are not the only ones John expresses using first person plural. We also have the perfect tense plural verbs *akēkoamen* (we have heard) in 1:2, 3; and *eōrakamen* (we have seen) in 1:1, 2, 3; in addition to the personal pronouns *hēmōn* (our or us—1:1, 3, 4), *hēmeis* (we—1:4), *hēmin* (to us—1:2) and *hēmetera* (our—1:3).

12. Plummer commenting on this says, "We have the testimony of the last survivor of those who had heard and seen the Lord, the sole representative of His disciples, speaking in their name" (1888: 14). Also see Ngewa 2003: 431.

more than necessary.¹³ However, given that one of his chief concerns is to show that what he writes is reliable,¹⁴ the plural to convey plurality of witnesses is more likely. The principle of two or three witnesses in matters of importance (Deut 17:6; 19:15) was something he was aware of.¹⁵ His point is that what is borne witness of and announced, as he writes this epistle, is something beyond doubt. The guide provided on such matters has been followed and so the matter established. It is left to the hearers themselves to accept or not accept the well-established fact.

John uses four sensory verbs, covering three senses (seeing, hearing, and touching) to assure the readers that the witness comes from deep personal experience. Three times (1:1, 2, 3) he uses *heōrakamen* (a perfect tense, "we have seen") and in one of them (1:1) adds *tois ophthalmois hēmōn* ("with our eyes"); the dative *tois ophthalmois* serving as dative of means and emphasizing that the witness is beyond doubt.¹⁶ The other three sensory verbs are *akēkoamen* (also a perfect, "we have heard") which he uses twice (1:1, 3), *etheasametha* (an aorist, "we beheld") found in 1:1, and *epsēlaphēsan* (an aorist, "they touched") in 1:1. The subject of the act of touching is *hai cheires hēmōn* ("our hands"), again added for emphasis. The witness is firsthand. It is "our eyes" that saw and it was "our hands" that touched.

---

13. The basic question is whether John is using plural here but actually means "I." This is possible, with the intention being that of using a "majestic/authoritative" or "editorial" plural. However, given that he has "we" for the witness bearers and "you" (plural) for the hearers/readers (see for example, *humin* in 1:3) it is quite reasonable to see him here as associating himself with others. These others could be his faithful readers, other eyewitnesses of Jesus' life and ministry in general, or the apostles specifically. Deciding between these possibilities is not a matter of life and death. What is most significant here is that what John says meets the standard of reliable witness. For a more detailed discussion on this debate, see Brown 1982: 158–61; Burdick 1985: 98; and Jobes 2014: 48–51. Smalley (1984: 8) well observes that we see John using the first person plural pronoun both in contexts where he is identifying himself with other guardians of the apostolic truth and also when he is associating himself with his readers.

14. This is very clear in view of his emphatic use of all the senses, as discussed below, in experiencing what he testifies about.

15. The same principle of multiple witnesses for an important matter was used by Jesus in Matt 18:16 and John 8:17–18, and by Paul in 2 Cor 13:1 and 1 Tim 5:19. In this epistle, the same principle is at play in 5:8.

16. There is no other part of the body used in seeing but "the eyes." Use of "we have seen" could have been enough. John, however, uses the pleonasm here to emphasize the fact. The use of "our" is also emphatic. It is our eyes, and not other persons' eyes on our behalf.

Reliable Testimony and Its Goal (1:1–4)

A question that arises naturally is why John uses two different tenses: perfect tense for hearing (*akēkoamen*) and seeing (*heōrakamen*[17]) but aorist tense for beholding (*etheasametha*) and touching (*epsēlaphēsan*). Some have seen some significance in this change. Stott, for example, views the perfect verbs as "suggesting the abiding possession which results from the hearing and seeing" while the aorist verbs "seem to refer to a particular time" specifically after the resurrection.[18] It is doubtful, however, that apostle John lays different weight to the two pairs of verb tenses. They may be understood the same way (as perfects) if the two aorist forms are viewed as resultative aorist.[19] This is why the NIV, for example, renders the four verbs as "have heard," "have seen," "have looked at," and "have touched."[20] The four actions have abiding result in the production of witnesses who not only saw but also heard and who not only beheld but also touched. All that is needed for a reliable witness is there. In addition, the witness is not by one person but by many as the use of the "we" and "our" communicate.

John uses two different verbs here to present the sense of sight. He uses *horan* three times (1:1, 2, 3) and *theasthai* once (1:1). It is possible that *theasthai* has some nuances that *horan* does not have. Burdick, for example, says that *theasthai* was brought into the picture here so as "to emphasize the careful, inspective kind of seeing with which the disciples examined the revelation of God in Jesus Christ."[21] The difference, however, is not to be stressed to the degree that the act of seeing (*horan*) becomes of less

---

17. The focus of the two perfect verbs here is more on the result (intensive shade) than the process of "hearing" and "seeing" (extensive shade). John wants his readers to know that he and other apostles were persons in whose lives these experiences were fully realized. They are not using guess work or quoting a theory.

18. Stott (1964: 60) identifies the particular time behind the aorist verbs here as "perhaps after the resurrection, when the apostles had an opportunity both to gaze thoughtfully upon the Lord Jesus and to handle him." See also, Westcott 1892: 5; Plummer 1888: 15; and Burdick 1985: 99.

19. The fact that the Greek language uses the aorist in a perfective or resultative sense is a well accepted observation (See, for example, Dana and Mantey 1957: 196; Moulton 1963: 72; Brooks and Winbery 1979: 100; Wallace 1996: 559; and Brown 1982: 161). This being the case, the use of the two tenses would here be merely a matter of literary variation with no exegetical difference. The degree and effect of the four actions are the same. John and his associates saw, heard, beheld, and touched and on basis of that experience now bear witness.

20. See also Holman Standard Christian Bible, New King James Bible, and Smalley 1984: 7.

21. Burdick 1985: 99. See also Stott 1964: 60; and Brooke 1912: 4.

significance in contributing to the witness here.²² The act of seeing (*horan*) cannot be devoid of careful examination in this context. It is who/what they saw (*heōrakamen*) that they proclaim (1:3). It cannot be less than accurately determined person and message.

The person and message they bear witness concerning, and announce, is presented as having been "from the beginning" (*ēn ap' archēs*) in 1:1, "with the Father" (*ēn pros ton patera*) in 1:2, and "revealed" (*ephanerōthē*—stated twice in 1:2). This kind of description gives the impression that John is here talking about Jesus, who is second Person of the Trinity.²³ If so, it raises the question why John uses the neuter pronoun *ho* rightly translated as "what" instead of the masculine *hos* (who). The more common view is that John uses the neuter relative so that he captures all that is included—combining the person, his message, and everything else about him together.²⁴ If the masculine *hos* was used, it would limit the reference to the person. If the feminine relative pronoun *hē* was used, it would limit it to the message (*angellia*). John chooses to use the neuter so that it would be all inclusive of the person and the message. Jobes' suggestion that the neuter may be used because the author is thinking of *euangelion* (gospel), which is neuter, or "the more abstract idea of the significance of Jesus' life, death, and resurrection"²⁵ could also be a possibility if it were not for the difficulties it faces as to how such would be seen and touched. The object of the verbs seem to be more personal than non-personal.

The two descriptions: "was from the beginning" (1:1) and "was with the Father" (1:2) place the person and message in eternity while "was revealed" (1:2) places the same in history. The person and message are both eternal and part of human history.

The "beginning" (*archē*) in question here precedes the beginning of Gen 1:1 (beginning of creation).²⁶ It parallels the beginning of the Gospel of

---

22. Smalley views the use of the two verbs as a matter of literary variation (1984: 8).

23. These same expressions are found in the Gospel of John 1:1, 14, and the context there is even clearer that it is Jesus who is meant.

24. Plummer says that John employs the neuter "as the most comprehensive expression to cover the attributes, words, and works of the Word and the Life manifested in the flesh" (1888: 14). Brown also, after observing that some of the verbs used (see and look) suggest a personal object while others (heard and proclaim) suggest impersonal object, concludes that the neuter refers to "the whole career of Jesus . . . functioning comprehensively to cover the person, the words, and the works" (1988: 154).

25. Jobes 2014: 43–44.

26. While there are other positions also (for example, the origin of the faith experience

Reliable Testimony and Its Goal (1:1–4)

John 1:1. It is a beginning that relates the existence of Jesus and all that his person entails with the existence of God. In other words, it is a beginning that moves out of history into eternity. On the other hand though, the eternal one was made manifest. It was in his state of "having been manifested" that John and his associates had the privilege of exercising their senses in knowing about him. Before they had contact with him he "was" already, and in their contact with him, he was "real." He is eternal God who became incarnate. John is not making these statements for the fun of it. He is cutting the roots of false teachers among his readers, as it will become clearer when he brings in the need of confession that Jesus is Son of God become flesh (2:22–23).[27]

The use of the imperfect *ēn* in the two phrases "was from the beginning" and "was with the Father" is significant from two fronts. First, the use of *einai* (of which *ēn* is an imperfect form) is generally distinct from *ginesthai*. While the latter carries with it the idea of a beginning or coming into existence,[28] *einai* assumes existence. Secondly, the tense used here is imperfect whose exegetical significance is "continuance in the past."[29] The point, therefore, is that the existence of the person John is talking of here was in continuance in the beginning, and so also was his fellowship with the Father.

We are further told in 1:1 that the content of the witness and announcement concerns "word of life" (*ho logos*[30] *tēs zōēs*), a life further defined as "the life eternal" (*tēn zōēn tēn aiōnion*) in 1:2. The use of *logos* is not new in the writings of John, for he uses the same for Jesus in John 1:1. The relation of "word" to its description "of life" (*tēs zōēs*) is either that he

---

of the witness bearers—Lieu 2008: 38) the context here, and especially the use of "what was," using a form of *eimi* and not *ginomai*, favors this position. Kruse rightly argues that each of John's ten uses of the expression "from beginning" in this epistle needs to be seen within its context (2000: 57).

27. The same is also a matter of concern in 2 John as seen in v. 7.

28. It is forms of *ginomai* that we find in such passages as John 1:14 (the word became flesh) and 1 John 2:18 (many antichrists have come into existence).

29. The shade of the imperfect here is durative/progressive imperfect. At that time referred to as beginning, the one in question existed and his fellowship with God (the Father) was a reality.

30. In the Greek text, this is also in the genitive, but this is because it accompanies the preposition *peri*. Thus, a genitive of reference.

(the word) gives life[31] or he himself is life.[32] Identification of Jesus as "life" is not far-fetched in view of Jesus' own claim in John 14:6: "I am the Way, the Truth, and the Life." Jesus gives life because he himself is Life.

By implication, therefore, we have here a reliable witness concerning one whose titles include "Word" and "Life"; one who is eternal, having his existence in continuance with the Father in the beginning; yet one who has been revealed. He is outside of history (since he is eternal) but has been made to become part of history (since he has been revealed). This is one of the distinguishing features of what John announces here, from other forms of beliefs.[33] There is combination in it of both eternity and time. During the phase of his life in which he was living on this earth, he was seen, heard, beheld, and touched. In his eternal existence, he was with the Father.

The goal of the activities of bearing witness and announcing is that the readers will also have fellowship with the writer and his team (*hina kai humeis koinōnian echēte meth' hēmōn*, "in order that you [yourselves] also may have fellowship with us," 1:3), whether the team is limited to the apostles[34] or includes all believers[35] that share the experience John expresses in the four sensory verbs. There are four levels of fellowship here.[36] First there is the fellowship John has with his fellow-apostles.[37] Then, there is the fellowship John is inviting his readers to have with him and the other apostles.

---

31. Taking *tēs zōēs* here as objective genitive.

32. Treating *tēs zōēs* as epexegetical or explanatory genitive.

33. When we talk of Islam, for example, we think of Mohammed its founder and we know he lived AD 570 to 632. When we talk of Buddhism, we think of Gautama Buddha who lived about 563 to 483 BC. Jesus Christ, however, the one John is pointing to as the center of his message, lived in eternity. The use of 4 or 5 BC as his birthdate is only in his "revealed" and not "eternal" existence.

34. See, for example, Westcott 1892: 12; and Kistemaker 1986: 237.

35. See, for example, Smalley 1984: 12.

36. The Greek word translated "fellowship" is *koinōnia*. It has the idea of a "living bond" (Hauck 1965: 807). There is a partnership that goes with the relationship. In this Epistle of John (1:3, 6, 7) the partnership is both in holy character (based on the holy character of God—1:5) as well as in ministry of proclaiming the news about the Word of life. John and his fellow apostles have become partners with God in his holiness and have become witnesses of it. He is inviting his readers to enjoy this blessing with him and his fellow apostles. It is a fellowship in a faith that accepts the incarnation of Christ and sees sin as it is (Schattenmann 1975: 634). There are, therefore, both theological and moral bases in this fellowship.

37. As John implies in the use of "we" throughout this section, John and his fellow-apostles are in agreement about what he writes concerning the Word of life. They are partners in bearing this news to the world.

Reliable Testimony and Its Goal (1:1–4)

John then adds a third fellowship, which is much more blessed than these horizontal ones (apostle with apostle and apostles with readers/hearers). Both the apostles and their readers who accept the invitation have a fellowship with the Father and the Lord Jesus Christ (1:3)[38] who themselves have been in fellowship with one another from the beginning, that is eternity (1:1). This is a wonderful community[39] of fellowship (*koinōnia*).

Where there is the fellowship John has in mind here, heart meets heart in the openness of sharing and sincere support of each other. It begins with those who are themselves "witness bearers" or "announcers." Using modern language, it starts with the ministers of the gospel. It does not dwell on whether one was a fisherman, tax collector, a tent maker, or whatever else our backgrounds are. It is a fellowship around the joy of salvation and the duty to announce it to others. The competition we see from time to time among those who bear the titles "pastor," "Bible teacher," or "bishop" is out of place. It fails miserably in reflecting the business they have been called to. There is eternal fellowship between the Father and the Son, which we are called upon to not only exemplify but also to announce and invite others to. It is a fellowship which leads us to "share all things in common" in the sense that none of us will starve while others feast. In our day, it is an international fellowship since we live in a global village. We are meant to rejoice together and to cry together, to eat together and to starve together—all hearts united to God to please him, and to each other in love. Nevertheless, and as John will show later in disputing some wrong teachings, the fellowship within the context of relationships has as its base the context of belief. This is why John relates this fellowship to the witness on whose bases the facts about the Word of life are reaffirmed. Schnackenburg rightly observes

---

38. Though mystical union is not as pronounced in 1 John as it is in Paul, it is not missing either. The ideas of being in Christ or God (2:5: we are in him; 2:24: you will remain in the Son and in the Father; 2:28: you, remain in him) and Christ or God being in the believer (3:24: in him he remains and he in him; 4:4: greater is the one in you; 4:13: we remain in him and he in us; 4:15: God remains in him and he in God; 4:16: he remains in God and God remains in him) capture the notion of mystical union all right.

39. There is the African traditional worldview captured by the statement "I am because you are" that is fading away very fast. On the day this note was being written (September 19, 2017) one of the major items in the news, in Kenya, were some young men who had set fire to the homes or businesses of others in their community leaving women and children helpless in the cold. In the past, the strength of the young was useful in defending the community. Now, in many cases, it is used to destroy or even kill. There is urgency in introducing the wonderful community John is talking about here. It centers on God who is love, and his Son who gave his own life because of love for us. Blessed are the feet whose primary business is to promote this fellowship!

that even in the forward, the author "focuses on the heresy he is combating throughout the letter."⁴⁰ This, however, should not be emphasized to the point where it becomes the controlling factor of John's message here. John's message is broader than just correcting the heresy. His message is not just corrective of error but much more a reaffirmation of a wonderful blessing that is ours as believers. We have a fellowship whose base is eternal, in the Trinity, and whose completion is achieved by inviting others to enjoy it. We, however, do so as a team, fellowshipping in life of holiness and purity of doctrine.

The readers' positive response to the witness borne and announcement made becomes an opportunity to increase the joy of the witness bearers. John says, "in order that our joy may have been made full or complete" (*hina hē chara hēmōn ē peplērōmenē*, 1:4). The use of the verb "complete" or "make full" (*plēroun*) is deliberate here, with regard to this joy. In other words, it is not that they do not have joy even before the readers' response. They do, on the basis of their own fellowship with God and Jesus Christ. Until the readers are brought in, however, there is still something missing. Here is a lesson for us. Yes, we need to enjoy the presence of God all the time. However, when we fail to invite others to enjoy that blessing also, the process is not complete. The duty of the believer is not to enjoy and store for oneself, but to enjoy and dispense the same to others, to enjoy also. It is a call to a mission that never ceases as long as we are in the world.

The literal translation of the periphrastic construction *ē peplērōmenē* in 1:4 is "may have been made complete,"⁴¹ that is, by the act of sharing and much more so by the positive response of the hearers. True Christian ministry means rejoicing when we see others grow in their faith. It is a fellowship that leaves out all competition and jealousies. We are not called to build our empires but to bring others to fellowship with God and other members of the community of faith. What a corrective reminder to us serving the Lord in the twenty-first century where we witness all sorts of unhealthy competitions for control and pursuit for personal fame and prosperity!

---

40. Schnackenburg 1992: 56.

41. The focus here is more the result (intensive perfect) than the process (extensive perfect).

Inescapable Fact and Its Implication (1:5–10)

> (1:5) And this is the message which we have heard from him and we announce to you, that "God is light and in him there is not any darkness at all."[42] (6) If we should say that we have fellowship with him while we walk in darkness, we lie and we do not do the truth (7) But if we should walk in the light as he himself is in the light, we have fellowship with one another and the blood of Jesus his Son cleanses us from every sin (8) If we should say that we do not have sin, we deceive ourselves and the truth is not in us (9) If we should confess our sins, he is so faithful and just that he will forgive[43] us the sins and will cleanse[44] us from every unrighteousness (10) If we should say that we have not sinned, we make him a liar and his word is not in us.

This passage revolves around an inescapable fact found in 1:5, namely, "God is light" (*ho theos phōs estin*). The verb "is" (*estin*) here makes an assertion that is true at all times. It is a timeless fact.[45] This is emphasized by saying the same thing in a different way in the same verse, that is, "and in him, there is not any darkness at all" (*kai skotia en autō ouk estin oudemia*). Within his being and the sphere in which God dwells, there is no darkness at all.

There is no doubt that "light" and "darkness" are used metaphorically here. Light may be viewed as standing for holiness while darkness stands for sin.[46] Simply put, therefore, one may say, "God is holy and in him there is no sin at all." At one level, sin may be defined as that which is contrary to the will of God, but at another level it can be defined as that which hurts

---

42. The Greek word translated "not at all" is *oudemia*, whose literal meaning (*ou-de-mia*) is "not even one." The point is that there is not even a single spot of darkness.

43. Taking the aorist subjunctive *aphē* here as proleptic aorist. It is made very certain by the nature of God, though it is still future in terms of its realization.

44. Taking the aorist subjunctive *katharisē* as proleptic aorist also.

45. The best way to take it here is as a gnomic present. God is not light today, as if he was not light yesterday or will not be light tomorrow. He was light when John wrote and He is light in the twenty-first century. His nature never changes, even with the changing of times.

46. This moral connotation of "light" and "darkness" is also found in other passages in 1 John. For example in 2:9–11, "being in the light" is spelled out as the dwelling sphere of the one who loves his brother or sister while "being in darkness" is the sphere of one who hates his brother or sister. "Loving" and "hating" are moral acts and they define the sphere one dwells in.

God's creation.[47] God made creation to live in harmony, but it was the intrusion of sin that destroyed that harmony. In the garden of Eden where sin entered into the sphere of humankind (Gen 3; Rom 5:12) there was disobedience for sure but much more so, there was hurt, embarrassment (Gen 3:7, 10) and passing of blame (Gen 3:12, 13). Life of joy, confidence, and oneness were taken away from Adam and Eve. Harmony was also taken away from the rest of creation (Gen 3:17, 18). The rule of God who is light restores this harmony between members of humankind, by way of fellowship with God and with one another.

A further point we can draw from this statement of fact (that is, God is light) is that God cannot deny himself or hurt any of his creation. He keeps his promises and is out to do good to all those prepared to benefit from his fellowship with them. This benefit must also be extended to all his creation. By implication, the Christian duty is not just toward God and to other members of humankind, but also to our environment and all the creation that surrounds us.

Conditions upon which such a relationship can be maintained are spelled out. They are expressed in such a way that they confront the one who assumes this relationship without reflecting on what the inescapable fact about God's holiness means. At the same time, they also affirm the faithfulness of God in dealing with those who walk in obedience to the will of God.

---

47. When God, following his creation, said "it was good" (Gen 1:4, 10, 12, 18, 21, 25) or "it was very good" (Gen 1:31), he meant that there was harmony between him and his creation, harmony within the souls and bodies of his creation, and harmony in the relationships of one creation toward the other. Entrance of sin disrupted all these levels of harmony. Christ came to restore this harmony. Our relationship with him determines our relationship with God, with each other, and even with all his creation. The believer is, therefore, not only called upon to relate well to God and to fellow human beings, but also to his or her environment. Even as all creation longs for the perfect order it will be brought back to (Rom 8:19–21) the believer is called upon to do his or her role in maintaining that order as a Christian responsibility. A believer who claims to love God and hates his brother or sister is a liar (1 John 4:20). By extension, so also a believer who deliberately fails to take care of the environment. The call for the believer is not only to restore relationship with God and other people, but also within creation in general. When a believer plants trees and as a result the chances for better rainfall follow, this is a service to God and his creation. On the contrary, when a believer encourages deforestation and lack of rain follows, he or she hurts God's creation. Life in Christ is an all-rounded responsibility.

Inescapable Fact and Its Implication (1:5–10)

Three situations are spelled out, hypothetically[48] presupposing the manner in which a critic could develop his or her argument to justify his or her behavior contrary to the nature of God. John raises the possible claim and then responds to it, so that the one who is in the wrong corrects his or her way and those who are in the right dig their feet deeper into what is right. Deliberately, John is attacking the false teaching step by step until the wise one has no choice but to correct his or her way, for there is no further argument to justify one's walk contrary to the will of God.

The first situation is a claim to have fellowship with God while at the same time walking in darkness (1:6). Logically, such a claim is dismissed by the inescapable fact that God is light. How can God in whom there is no darkness at all have fellowship with someone walking in darkness? The two are as far apart as opposite poles of the universe. The verb translated "walking" is in the present tense, meaning it is the habit of such a person. Person of complete holiness and another of habitual sin cannot have fellowship. John says that such a person lies[49] and does not do the truth (1:6b). Using the first person plural, since this would apply to anyone who makes such a claim, he says, "we lie [to ourselves] and do not do the truth" (*pseudometha kai ou poioumen tēn alētheian*). Not doing the truth is a statement of enforcement to "lying." It says the same thing in a different way. Such a claim is an act of "lie" and not an act of "truth."

The "lying" and "not doing" the truth also are expressed using the present tense. Treating them both as iterative present, the idea would be that whenever we make such a claim, it amounts to cheating ourselves and not living out what is factual. It is not a judgment about our nature but a statement about the result of a claim that does not meet the qualifications. We can be believers who have been transformed by the blood of Christ but are not living up to expectation. The call would then not be "to conversion" but "to live out a life of the converted." This is a message for all of us. We must walk out our nature, and our nature is based on the nature of God, which is total holiness. From what John writes and how he argues it out,

---

48. The use of "hypothetical" here does not preclude that John's argument was dictated by what was on the ground. It is used to guard from a definite conclusion that there was someone arguing at three levels on the matter. What seems obvious is that there was some downplaying of sin and its seriousness.

49. The literal meaning is "lies" because the verb is a middle deponent. However, it is not out of order to perceive this lying as to oneself first—that is, the one who makes such a claim is lying to himself or herself. John's point is that it will not work even if the one making the claim attempts to convince him- or herself that there is fellowship.

there must have been some who tended to belittle the matter of sin. When God's nature is called into the picture, sin is excluded in all its forms and degree. This is not a message for then (John's time) only but also for us who live in the twenty-first century. Times may change and advancements may be made on many fronts like science and philosophies, but God's nature never changes from being light to being darkness. This needs to be the glasses through which believers of all centuries examine the trends of their times.

To avoid refuting the claim and not give a positive statement, John goes on to indicate what blessings are ours if we walk in the light as God is in the light (1:7). The blessings include fellowship with one another (*koinōnian echomen met' allēlōn*, "we have fellowship with one another") and cleansing from every sin by Jesus' blood (*to haima Iesou tou hyiou autou katharizei hēmas apo pasēs hamartias*, "the blood of Jesus his Son cleanses us from every sin"). Those who walk in the light are not only in God's likeness but are also like-minded.[50] Persons who are like-minded live in harmony with each other. This state may not be one of perfection in relationships, but whenever there is a failure, it is followed by confession and, as a result, a cleansing from sin and movement forward.[51] The community of faith is expected to be on the move toward glorification. This is possible as we walk in the light, enjoy our fellowship with each other, and deal with sin whenever it occurs, through cleansing of Jesus' blood.

Members of humankind, in many parts of the world, are experiencing some degree of enmity with each other. Some areas have conflicts that have lasted for many years and the end of such conflicts does not seem to be in sight. Relating properly to God who is light, and seeking to do his will, is key to bringing about fellowship among members of humankind. The believers are called upon to set the example since they have a continuing fellowship with God the Father and God the Son (1:3). This fellowship is then lived out in our daily interaction with each other.

The second situation John refutes is the claim not to have sin (1:8). Again, using the first person plural he responds to the ones who may make the claim "we do not have sin" (*hamartian ouk echomen*). It is like John is

---

50. The tense of the verb "we have" is a present tense, best taken here as perfective present. It tells us the status in which we are placed by life of obedience. It is the status of harmony with God and with others.

51. The tense of the verb "cleanses" is another present tense, best taken as iterative. Whenever that which is perfect has not been attained, we are not left in a helpless situation. There is the provision of cleansing.

Inescapable Fact and Its Implication (1:5–10)

imagining that the critic he is dealing with here will respond to his mention of our sins being cleansed with a statement that he or she does not have sin to be cleansed. John points out that such a claim is self-deception (*heautous planōmen*, "we deceive ourselves") and lack of truth (*hē alētheia ouk estin en hēmin*, "the truth is not in us"). Just as the one who makes the first claim above is lying to self, so also the one who makes this second claim. Instead of repeating that such a person does not do the truth, however, John intensifies the situation as he says, the truth is not in such person. It is not only that the act is not according to the truth but also the total character is one that lacks truth.

Upon refuting this claim, John provides the positive statement, "if we confess our sins, God is faithful and righteous" (1:9) and will give to us the blessings of forgiveness (*hina aphē hēmin tas hamartias*, "that he will forgive us, with reference to the sins"[52]) and cleansing from unrighteousness (*kai katharisē hēmas apo pasēs adikias*, "and will cleanse us from every unrighteousness"). The Greek word translated "confess" is *homologeō* and it means, "I say as it is." It does not leave room for beating about the bush. It is a confession whose basis is clear knowledge of God's nature as light. When there is such knowledge, our response becomes like that of Isaiah as recorded in Isa 6:5. Those who open themselves, exposing the nakedness of their souls before God, always receive his forgiveness. The forgiveness is not based on how big or small the act of sin is. It is based on our humble confession, which then receives response from faithful and righteous God.

Describing God as faithful asserts that he keeps what he promises. We do not approach him just to find that he changed his mind on what he has promised. He is also righteous. He does what is right. He would never punish anyone for doing right or approve an act of sin. His deeds and his nature are consistent at all times.

The third and final claim John refutes here is the claim not to have sinned (*ouch hēmartēkamen*, "we have not sinned") found in 1:10. The situation is one in which after John has indicated the availability of forgiveness, the critic responds by saying that no act of sin has been committed so as to be forgiven. John sees two problems with such a claim: (1) we make God a liar, and (2) the word of God is not in us. The Scripture is very clear on the matter of all those who have been born by Adam and Eve (and this includes

---

52. The Greek here allows for two possibilities: taking the dative *hēmin* as dative of possession and so render the phrase "our sins" or take it as dative of direct object (both of them acceptable shades of the dative case with the verb *aphiēmi*) rendering it as "forgive us" and then treat the accusative *tas hamartias* as accusative of reference.

all members of humankind) being participants in sin. They are not only sinners by way of their own individual acts of sin (sin being defined as all that does not measure to the level of God's perfect nature as light) but also by virtue of having the touch of Adam and Eve—the grandparents of all of us. Theological debates may not be settled whether this passing on of sin from Adam and Eve to us is by way of representation or other,[53] but the fact that the sin has been passed on is expressed in the Bible without ambiguity (Pss 14:2, 3; 51:5; 130:3; 143:2; Rom 3:10–18; 5:12). To make the claim that one has not sinned, therefore, amounts to saying that God tells lies and also a failure to listen to the word of God. There is no escape except by way of confessing our sins. When confession has been done, forgiveness from faithful and righteous God is guaranteed. What an opportunity to enjoy fellowship with God, even from our weak point!

Summary of the Three Claims Refuted

The Claim	Consequences	Remedy	Blessings	Verses
Fellowship with God while living in darkness	Lie to ourselves

Not do the truth | Walk in the light | Fellowship with one another

Cleansing from sin | 1:6, 7 |
| We do not have sin | Deceive ourselves

Truth not in us | Confess sins | Forgiveness

Cleansing from unrighteousness | 1:8, 9 |
| We have not sinned | Make God a liar

His word not in us | – | – | 1:10 |

---

53. How Adam and Eve's act of sin becomes ours has been variously expressed. Two of the more common views include: representative view (Adam and Eve represented us and so when they sinned, we also sinned) and seminal view (we were all in Adam and Eve organically when they sinned).

The Intended Goal—Not to Sin (2:1–6)

(2:1) My little children, I write these things to you in order that you might not sin. And if anyone should sin we have an advocate with the Father, Jesus Christ the righteous; (2) and he (himself) is a propitiation for our sins, and not for ours only but also for the whole world. (3) And by this we know that we have known him, if we keep his commandments. (4) The one who says, "I have known him" and does not keep his commandments, is a liar, and the truth is not in him; (5) but whoever keeps his word, truly in him the love of God has been perfected. By this we know that we are in him; (6) the one who claims to remain in him ought also to walk just as he himself walked.

After addressing his readers as "my little children" (*teknia mou*) in 2:1, John tells them the reason for his writing as "in order that you might not sin" (*hina mē hamartēte*). The use of the aorist tense here (*hamartēte*) could be deliberate, to communicate that his purpose for writing is that the readers would not do an act of sin.[54] Elsewhere in the epistle, John uses present tense verbs as he disassociates the believer from sin. In 3:6, using the present tense *hamartanei*, he says, "Everyone who remains in him does not sin" (*pas ho en autō menōn ouch hamartanei*), and in 3:9 uses both the present tenses *poiei* and *hamartanein* as he says, "Everyone who has been born of God does not do sin . . . is not able to sin" (*pas ho gegennēmenos ek tou theou hamartian ou poiei . . . ou dunatai hamartanein*). As it will be shown when these passages are discussed below, John is asserting that a believer cannot sin as a matter of habit. In his use of aorist tense in 2:1, he is seeing the goal of obeying God's word as freedom from sin. However, John cannot by this assertion be denying that even the believer has the inherited sinful nature. If he said this, he would be denying his own statement in 1:8. The point rather is that the believer and sin belong to two different spheres. This is in view of who God is (light, and in him there is no sin—1:5) and who believers are (persons in fellowship with God—1:3). Sin is, therefore, not to be perceived as mere disobedience to some set of rules, but a failure to respond in any given situation in a manner that corresponds to God being light.[55]

---

54. While a mere use of aorist tense cannot be taken as communicating one act, that thought is also expressed by the use of the aorist tense as contrasted with the use of the present or imperfect tenses.

55. Yarbrough 2008: 75.

John hastens to acknowledge that total freedom from sin may not be a possible experience in this life and so pronounces provision for that act of sin, which a believer may find it to be his or her experience from time to time. He states, in 2:1b, "and if anyone should sin, we have an advocate with the Father" (*kai ean tis hamartē, paraklēton echomen pros ton patera*). His work as our advocate[56] is that he stands in our place so that we are not consumed by the holy God. He stood for us on the cross, and on the basis of the blood he shed to cleanse our sins (1:9) he stands even now when we sin and confess that sin.[57] John identifies this advocate as "Jesus Christ the righteous." The use of the adjective "righteous" (*dikaios*) here is important. It is because he has no case of his own[58] to answer before the court of heaven that he can serve as our advocate. At a secondary level, the quality of being righteous can also be applied to the manner in which he dispenses his services. He does not only qualify before God who is light, but also serves his clients (us) faithfully. We at times hear of advocates who have not passed on to their clients whatever the courts of justice awarded to them. Not advocate Jesus Christ! As Yarbrough puts it, "There is no chance that what he urges in God's presence will be rejected" and "those who look to him for advocacy can be assured that he will do the right thing."[59]

56. The Greek word, *paraklētos*, is a Johannine term. In the Gospel of John (14:16, 26; 15:26; 16:7) Jesus uses it of the Holy Spirit, describing him as "another comforter" in 14:26. He is another in that Jesus has been their *paraklētos* and now he is leaving them. The other *paraklētos* will encourage them and it is on this basis that their hearts should not be troubled (14:1). Here (1 John 2:1), John uses it for Jesus and in the context of dealing with sin. It is a word whose meaning is tied to the context and purpose for which the person so described comes alongside. It could be comfort as in John 14:16 or for intercession or defense as in 1 John 2:1. Both comforter and advocate are appropriate translations.

57. When I first heard someone talk of "my doctor" or "my lawyer," I thought that they had a doctor or lawyer that was exclusively employed by them. With time, however, I got to know that such descriptions are for some qualified person we have chosen to visit when we are unwell or are in need of legal counsel. In the same way, Jesus is "our advocate." He presents our cases before the holy God, lest his perfect holiness deals harshly with us as sinful people. Just as there is a problem when we are sick and we have no doctor, or we need legal counsel and we have no lawyer, so also it is when we want to deal with holy God without letting Jesus be our advocate. Not acknowledging Jesus' importance in our lives is a misunderstanding of God's nature. He is holy and demands holiness from his creation.

58. Peter (1 Pet 1:19) describes him as lamb without blame and in 1 Pet 2:22 as one who committed (using the aorist tense *epoiēsen*) no sin.

59. Yarbrough 2008: 77. In his commenting, Yarbrough says, "While Jesus's death has the effect of expiating sin (wiping away its penalty), it is difficult to avoid the impression

The Intended Goal—Not to Sin (2:1–6)

In 2:2 John further describes Jesus as "propitiation for our sins" (*hilasmos . . . peri tōn hamartiōn hēmōn*). The meaning of the term *hilasmos* is debated. It is, for example, translated propitiation here (also, NKJB and NASB), expiation (NRSV), or sacrifice of atonement (NIV). The basis of the debate is that the word propitiation focuses on the fact that God is appeased (and by implication he was wrathful), while expiation focuses on sins' removal, tying it especially with the function of the mercy seat[60] within the Old Testament's economy of redemption. The NIV's choice (sacrifice of atonement) could be influenced by the fact that both ideas are facts, in view of Scripture. God's wrath against sin is real (Rom 1:18) and removal of sin (1:9) is the act by which God's attitude changes from one of wrath to that of fellowship with the believer. While the context here seems to favor more the act of appeasing God (it goes well with his work as advocate) the idea of expiation should not be totally lost. It is because sins have been removed that God is appeased. These intertwined functions make Yarbrough translate the term (*hilasmos*) as "expiatory propitiation."[61] One of them (expiation) is basis of the other (propitiation) and the other is a guaranteed outcome of the first.

John says that the sins in question here is not only our (believers') but *peri holou tou kosmou* ("for the whole world"). Jesus died for me in particular and for everyone else in general. As commonly put in theology, the death of Jesus was and is sufficient for every sin, but only efficient for sins that are confessed. It is the basis upon which God has extended, and continues to extend, "patience and forbearance to those who merit his rejection."[62] It satisfied the demands against everyone who comes by faith to accept him as *hilasmos* (basis for removal of sin and restoration of fellowship with God).

With the matter made clear who Jesus is to us as believers (that is, *paraklētos* and *hilasmos*) John goes on to state how our knowledge of him may be tested. It is "if we keep his commandments" (*ean tas entolas autou tērōmen*, 2:3). In fact, John continues and says that the one who claims this knowledge and does not keep his commandments "is a liar and the truth

---

that it also propitiates (turns away the wrath of) God's promised punishment of sin and sinners whose sins are not atoned for" (Yarbrough 2008: 78).

60. The word translated as "mercy seat" is in the LXX *hilastērion*, a cognate of *hilasmos*.

61. Yarbrough 2008: 77.

62. Yarbrough 2008: 79.

is not in him" (*pseustēs estin kai en toutō hē alētheia ouk estin*, 2:4). This is because the commandments are rooted in the will of God and the provision of Jesus as advocate and propitiation is part of that will. To know Jesus means that we will seek to do the will of God, which in summary is to be like Christ. The knowledge spoken of here is not just "knowledge about" but "knowledge in experience."[63] One cannot have close experience with God through Jesus and still disregard the importance of keeping his commandments. This may not mean perfection, but the heart's determination to please God. Such determination causes us to confess any imperfection that sets into our lives. It is such determination that makes the Scriptures describe David as a man after God's heart (Acts 13:22, quoting 1 Sam 13:14) even when we know that he failed miserably at some point (2 Sam 11). God does not deal with us in wrath when we have not achieved perfection, so long as our hearts strive for perfection because he is our God.

On the other hand is the one who keeps the commandments (2:5a). John uses "whoever" (*hos an*) to imply that God does not shut anyone out of the blessings that go with the act of keeping the commandments. Concerning such a person, John says, "truly in him the love of God has been perfected" (*alēthōs en toutō hē agapē tou theou teteleiōtai*). While the genitive *tou theou* (of God), describing love, could be the love that God has toward such a person (subjective genitive[64]) or even a love like that which God exercises (qualitative genitive[65]), it is better to treat it here as the love the person who keeps God's commandments has toward God (objective genitive).[66] Later on (see under 2:15) John contrasts our love for the world and our love for the Father (using another genitive, *hē agapē tou patros*— "the love of the Father") and is in order to treat it here (2:5) in the same way. At least, there is nothing within the context here that makes that choice

---

63. Of the two major Greek words for the idea of knowing, *oida* may have as its focus the knowledge at the level of facts, while *ginōskō* has as its focus, knowledge at the experiential level. For example, one may know that sugar is sweet because he/she has read it from a text book. It is knowledge of a different level when one has placed sugar in his/her mouth and states "sugar is sweet." One may know Jesus at the level of facts without knowing him at the level of experience. John argues that one cannot know Jesus at the level of experience and not keep the commandments. The essence of Christian faith or theological studies is not achieved with mere study of facts, no matter how well those facts have been grasped. The knowledge of facts must lead to the knowledge at experience level for the Christian mission to be complete.

64. See Lieu 2008: 71.

65. See Schnackenburg 1992: 97.

66. See also Yarbrough 2008: 86; and Kruse 2000: 88.

The Intended Goal—Not to Sin (2:1–6)

unviable. Using human illustration here, when one tells another person "I love you" it is appreciated. However, it is not complete until the statement has been applied in actual life situations. In the same way also, the one who says he or she loves God. That claim must be made full or perfect by pleasing God, the object of that love.[67] It is by loving God that we can be assured that we remain in him (2:5b). Our mystical union with God is based on clearly set conditions: keeping his commandments[68]—a natural outcome of knowledge, and appreciation of who Jesus is.

John finishes the section with a specific instruction (2:6) for anyone who claims to remain in this fellowship with God and Jesus Christ. He says that such a person "ought to walk[69] just as he himself walked"[70] (*opheilei kathōs ekeinos periepatēsen kai autos [houtōs] peripatein*). This is a clear statement of our need to pursue Christlikeness. Jesus conducted himself before the Father and in relationship to human beings in a manner that was all pure. Remaining in this fellowship means conducting ourselves in the same manner. Should this be achieved, it would be a life of sinlessnes (which John, in 2:1, said was his goal for writing). Since our experiences tell us that we still have to wait for glorification of our beings before we attain perfection, what we can confidently affirm is to seek to be like Christ. When we fail, Jesus is our advocate and we will be given a second chance. Perfection, however, is our goal and the march must always be on.

---

67. Another possible way of understanding this perfecting of love is seeing it as a process. The process began with God loving us, was followed by our loving God, and needs to be completed by our loving others. This would need to take the genitive "of God" (*tou theou*), qualifying love, as qualitative genitive. However, seeing it as a movement from a claim to actual demonstration of that claim in an act of obedience seems easier to comprehend. Where there is no obedience, there is no proof of love.

68. Though not pronounced in this context, we do know that for John, love toward God extends itself to love for other people (1 John 4:19). It would, therefore, not be far-fetched to also see John's point here as that the love God has loved us with (taking *tou theou* as subjective genitive) and responded to by us in loving him back (taking *tou theou* as objective genitive) is perfected by extending this kind of love (*agape*, taking *tou theou* as qualitative genitive) to fellow human beings. The commandments in view here would therefore anticipate the commandment of love John brings out in the following verses.

69. A present tense is used for the infinitive "to walk." It is to be our way of life, as a matter of habit.

70. The aorist tense here *periepatēsen* is a constative aorist. It covers the whole period Jesus dwelt among us, identifying with us in every way except in the area of sinning. He set an example of what it means to live in a Godward manner, even though living in this world.

Christ's walk of perfect obedience was crowned with death, on our behalf, on the cross. This was the highest degree of expression of love (John 10:11; 15:13; 1 John 3:16). It is not surprising, therefore, that this statement ushers in the theme of love among followers of Christ.

The Ageless Commandment—Old Yet New (2:7–17)

(2:7) Beloved ones, I do not write to you a new commandment but an old commandment which you have had from beginning; the commandment which is old is the word which you heard. (8) Again, a new commandment I write to you, which is true in him and in you, because darkness is passing away and the light which is true is shining already. (9) The person who claims to be in the light and hates his brother (or sister) is in darkness until now. (10) The one who loves his brother (or sister) remains in the light and there is no stumbling block in him or her (11) but the one who hates his brother (or sister) is in darkness and in darkness he (or she) walks and has not known where he (or she) is going, because the darkness has blinded[71] his (or her) eyes.

(12) I write to you, children,
   because your sins have been forgiven on account of his name
(13) I write to you fathers,
   because you have known the one from the beginning
I write to you young men,
   because you have overcome the evil one.
(14) I write[72] to you children,
   because you have known the Father.
I write to you fathers,
   because you have known the one from the beginning.
I write to you young men,
   because you are strong
      and the word of God remains in you
      and you have overcome the evil one.

(15) Do not love the world nor the things in the world. If anyone loves the world, the love of the Father is not in him (16) because everything in the world, the lust of the flesh, the lust of the

---

71. Taking the aorist tense *etyphlōsen* as a resultative aorist.
72. Taking the aorist *egrapsa* here as epistolary aorist.

The Ageless Commandment—Old Yet New (2:7-17)

eyes and the pride of life, is not of the Father but is of the world (17) And the world and its lusts pass away, but the person who does the will of God remains forever.

Having mentioned the need to keep God's commandments (2:3-6) John now focuses on one of these commandments, namely, the commandment of love. Two objects are the focus of the love John is writing to promote here. There is the love toward a brother or sister (contrasted with hating) and there is the love toward the Father (contrasted with love of the world and what goes with it)

Love Toward a Brother or Sister

After addressing his readers as "beloved" (*agapētoi*)[73] in 2:7a, John goes on to tell them that he is writing to them about a commandment. He gives the commandment the qualities of being both old (2:7) and new (2:8). It is old because his readers have had it from the beginning[74] (*hēn eichete ap' archēs*) and is by definition the word which they had already heard (*hē entolē hē palaia estin ho logos hon ēkousate*). At the same time, it is new (2:8). Its newness is most likely to be seen in the example of Christ[75] who John has described as *hilasmos* for our sins (2:2). Jesus himself said that there is no

---

73. John uses the term *agapētoi* for his readers of 1 John six times (2:7; 3:2, 21; 4:1, 7, 11). Its first occurrence in the New Testament is in the context of Jesus' baptism (Matt 3:17) where God the Father says concerning Jesus, *houtos estin ho hyios mou ho agapētos* (this is my Son, the beloved one). It has the idea of endearment. John deliberately uses it of his readers for them to know that he writes what he does because he cares about them. It is only because his readers are his *agapētoi* that he can convincingly encourage them to exercise *agapē* (love) toward each other.

74. The beginning here could include, beginning in the sense of God's revelation to his people (Lev 19:18: "love your neighbor as yourself"), in the sense of Jesus' ministry (John 13:34-35; 15:12: "Love each other as I have loved you"), or even in the sense of the readers' experience as believers. All these can be fitted into the understanding here, but the focus needs to be on the last one, in view of the readers having been participants in hearing it. The aorist verb *ēkousate*, whether taken in a constative sense (you heard) or in a resultative sense (you have heard) draws attention to the readers' participation.

75. John describes the relationship of the believer to Christ as one of being "in each other." Christ is in the believer and the believer is in Christ (3:24). While Christ demonstrated objectively what it means to love, he continues to work in the believer (subjectively) to bring the character of "loving as Christ did." It is an exercise that receives renewal at any time one reflects on Christ's example of love. Just as the hymn "Tis old yet ever new" describes the truth of the word of God, so also does it capture the idea of learning from Christ daily: walking as he walked (2:6).

greater love than one laying down his or her life for another (John 15:13). As *hilasmos*, Jesus did exactly this and so remains a supreme example of the act of love. John says that the practice of this commandment is true in Jesus and in the readers.[76] He gives the basis for this conclusion as that darkness is passing away and the true light is already shining (2:8b). Jesus had said that he is the light[77] of the world (John 9:5) and the readers have him as their Savior and Lord and so are living in his light. Where that light is in charge, there is love and not hatred. John writes to enhance this love as he encourages his readers to live in fellowship with God who is also described as light (1:5).

John moves on to give a clue as to what commandment he is talking about here by responding to the possible claim[78] of being in the light and not loving a brother or sister (2:9–11). The one who hates his brother or sister "is in darkness (*en tē skotia estin*[79]—repeated in 2:9, 11) until now" (*heōs arti*), even when he or she claims to be in the light. He or she is not only in darkness (sphere) but also "walks in darkness" (*kai en tē skotia peripatei*) and "does not know where he or she is going" (*kai ouk oiden pou hupagei*). The hating here is a continual practice (present tense *misōn*), the walking a continual act (present tense *peripatei*), and the ignorance a current status (the perfect tense *oiden*, used with the negative particle *ouk*). John gives the basis for the present status of such a person as that "the darkness has blinded[80] his eyes" (*hoti hē skotia etuphlōsen tous ophthalmous autou*). If the

---

76. Jesus did not only die to satisfy the demands of the law (being our *hilasmos*) but also to set an example for the believer to follow. The readers are not called only to know about Christ but also to be like him. The head is not the end, but the heart is. Intellectual understanding must be followed by the heart's response. As the believer follows the example of Christ of love, darkness in the form of hatred passes away. John is categorical that the one who hates his brother or sister lives in darkness (2:9) while the one who loves his brother or sister is in the light (2:10).

77. One of the functions of light is to show or point the way. Jesus as Light pointed out the way of love. This is why he tells his disciples, "Love as I loved you" (John 15:12). In other words, "I have defined *agapē* love in the way I have lived with you. You know what it means; now live it out."

78. John introduces the section with the words *ho legōn* (the one who says). This is a repeated phrase in this chapter (2:4, 6, 9) and it brings the idea that there is a claim implied.

79. The verb "to be" here, *estin*, is a durative present, with "until now" that follows emphasizing that this progressive condition is the *status quo* even as John writes.

80. Though an aorist is used in the Greek, the translation "has blinded" (taking it as resultative aorist) captures the idea well here. The eyes have been blinded and the outcome of the action remains—making it impossible for the one in question to see.

The Ageless Commandment—Old Yet New (2:7–17)

act of hating puts one into the sphere of darkness (2:9) and in God there is no darkness (1:5), it means that the one who hates is not in God's company. He or she has not known that the Christian walk is one of light (here shown by loving) and its destination is the city of holiness (Rev 21:22–27). The one who hates is not ready for heaven. Darkness clouds his or her eyes not to see the beauty of walking with God, enjoying his fellowship now and in eternity.

So as not to appear to be talking to only the person who makes the unacceptable claim, John also affirms the one who loves[81] (2:10). The one who loves (as a habit, present tense *agapōn*) his brother (or sister) remains in the light (continual status) and in him is no stumbling block (another continual status). The stumbling block is that which can trip him or her from living in fellowship with God and with others.[82] John's words here are like calling to mind the verse "love covers a multitude of sins" (Prov 10:12; 1 Pet 4:8). When we love someone, we shall not do him or her harm of any kind. Love serves as a catalyst to keep us in the light, which is God's sphere of existence.

While in 2:7–11 John tells his readers what he is writing to them, in 2:12–14 he tells them why he is writing (see discussion of this below). In summary, they have the qualification needed so as to be able to absorb what he is saying into their character. This is an important point because a repetition of the love commandment to a people who do not have that potential amounts to wasting of time. It is only the believer who can exercise the kind of love John is talking about here. It is a love that does not categorize people into classes for purpose of excluding some from love, not even into

---

81. The act of love is presented in the Greek using different words. There is the love that is equivalent to desire and even lust, based on what one will get from the exercise. This is captured in the word *eros*. There are then the acts of loving whose basis is a family relationship (*storgē*) or shared likes and dislikes (*philia*). The fourth word is *agapē* and that is the one we find throughout this epistle. It is a love that takes as first principle, what it will give away and not what it will get. It is a love that is uncommon except by those who determine to walk as Christ walked. Jesus said that he came to give his life as a ransom for many (Matt 20:28, Mark 10:45). Those who exercise this kind of love are truly the children of God.

82. The Greek word used is *skandalon* and it can mean a trap (snare) that causes one to fall or a stumbling block that causes someone else to fall. The idea of a trap seems to fit here more smoothly. The person talked about is walking in the light, his or her heart is full of love for others and consequently responds in a holy manner to difficult situations or people. In him or her, there is nothing that will become a trap, hindering his or her progress forward in the journey of Christ likeness.

"enemies" and "friends" categories (Matt 5:43–48) and it is a love that permeates every aspect of one's life.

John now addresses his readers using three classifications: little children (*teknia*, 2:12a), fathers (*pateres*, 2:13a), and young men (*neaniskoi*, 2:13b), which he repeats in 2:14 using the same classification except he now uses *paidia* and not *teknia* for children. These three verses (2:12–14) raise some interesting exegetical questions, including:

1. Are the classifications of children (*teknia, paidia*), fathers (*pateres*), and young men (*neaniskoi*) pointing to their level in physical age or in spiritual maturity, if either of the two?

2. Is there a difference between the two Greek words John uses for children here? That is, are *teknia* and *paidia* synonymous or does each have its own focus?

3. Why does John repeat the content of 2:12–13 in 2:14, with some of what he says to the group being exactly the same in both cases?

4. Why does he use the present tense, *graphō*, in the first set (2:12–13) and aorist tense, *egrapsa*, in the second set in 2:14?

Concerning the classification into children, fathers, and young men, the majority of scholars view these to be classification on their stage in Christian experience.[83] The "children" represents those who have been born into the Christian faith recently (probably both *teknia* and *paidia* being used for this group) or have not moved far in their spiritual growth even if they have had many years of belonging to the family of God. The young men represent those believers whose lives show clear evidence of victory in facing temptations and trials, while the fathers represent those who have many years of experience walking in the path of wisdom and fear of God.[84] They have come to know and teach that the fear of the Lord is the

---

83. Exceptions to this position are those scholars who see these classifications as referring to physical age, whether in three groups (children, young men, and fathers) or two, if "the children" is taken as including everyone in view of John's use of children for "all" elsewhere (2:1, 18 etc.). Plummer, who sees "children" as all inclusive but "young men" and "fathers" denoting physical age, describes them as "men in the prime, or not yet in the prime of life" and "older men," respectively (1888: 48). Also, see Haas et al. 1972: 54–55; and Kruse 2000: 93.

84. Stott 1964: 96; Bruce 1970: 58; Gorder 1978: 73–78.

The Ageless Commandment—Old Yet New (2:7-17)

beginning of wisdom (Prov 1:7) and can counsel others about the same on basis of their experience.[85]

Another approach, still under the spiritual experience classification, is to view the use of "children" (both *teknia* and *paidia*) as standing for all believers and the "young men" and "fathers" representing two levels in spiritual growth.[86] Brown,[87] who supports this position, sees the beauty of it as that once the entire community has been addressed as children (in both sets) the order of "fathers" and "young men" follows naturally (as opposed to the order: "children," "fathers," and "young men" if one took it to be three groups). To this can also be added the observation that John uses both *teknia* and *paidia* in contexts in which it is the whole community in view (2:1, 18, 28; 3:7, 18; 4:4; 5:21).[88] However, the use of a word in different senses within the same document is not an impossibility. For example, John can use *teknia* as all inclusive in some passages (see above) while in a different context use it as distinct from other groups. Here, he uses it alongside *neaniskoi* (young men) and *pateres* (fathers) and this could be an indicator of a different usage from places where it includes all believers.

As for the use of the two Greek words for children, *teknia* and *paidia*, it seems like John is using them interchangeably to refer to all his readers. He uses *teknia* in 2:1, 28; 3:7, 18; 4:4; and 5:21 in a manner that parallels his use of *paidia* in 2:18. If this be the case, and it is reasonable that it is, we can also say that it is the same group of people he has in mind when he uses the two words in this passage (2:12 and 2:14) though now using it specifically for those who have come to faith recently so that he can draw attention also to those who have been growing spiritually for sometime, that is the *neanisikoi* and the *pateres*. John is probably using the two (*teknia* and *paidia*) for

---

85. The position that the three classifications here are a simplification of "the standard categories of age and of participation in civic life in ancient society" (Lieu 2008: 87) may not be the case since the qualifications attached to each in this passage seems to correspond well with spiritual development of a believer. Lieu makes note of the seven stages found in Philo (*paidion* = the little child, up to age 7; *pais* = the child, up to age 14; *meirakion* = the youth, up to age 21; *neaniskos* = the young man, up to age 28; *anēr* = the man, up to age 49; *presbytēs* = the elder, up to age 56; and *gerōn* = the old man). This is a helpful observation but John may be simply acknowledging that in every congregation, there are different levels in spiritual maturity.

86. Examples of those who take this position include Kistemaker 1986: 266; Smalley 1984: 72; Westcott 1892: 58–60; Brooke 1912: 43; Burdick 1985: 182; Brown 1988: 112; Schnackenburg 1992: 116; and Kruse 2000: 88.

87. Brown 1982: 298.

88. See Kruse 2000: 88.

purpose of minimizing monotony, just as he may be doing in changing the tense from present to aorist (see discussion below). The dictionary[89] meaning for the two words are "little child" for *paidion* (being diminutive of, and related to *pais* which covers ages of 7–14 years) and "little child" for *teknion* (being a diminutive of and related to *teknon*, which sees it from the standpoint of origin or birth). The contextual meaning seems to support this interchangeability in meaning. If there is any slight difference to be drawn between the two, it may simply be that *teknion* does not only communicate the "littleness" but also denotes affection. Moulton and Milligan note that *teknon*, of which *teknion* is a diminutive, may also be used "as a form of kindly address, even in the case of grown-up persons."[90] Jesus used *teknia* for his disciples in John 13:33 and it is the same word (*tekna*) that is used when reference is made to believers as belonging to the family of God (5:2).

The repetition of the thoughts here in two pairs of three is striking. For the "fathers," for example, he repeats in 2:14 exactly what he said to them in 2:13: "you have known the one from (the) beginning" (*egnōkate ton ap' archēs*) and for the young men he says exactly the same thing in 2:13 and 2:14: "you have overcome the evil one" (*nenikēkate ton ponēron*). It is not strange for John, as a Jew, to be repeating these thoughts for the purpose of emphasis. This was a feature of a Jewish style of communication of matters that need to be stressed. Describing this passage as the "most rhetorically structured" Jobes sees the passage as patterned after Hebrew parallelism.[91] Lieu also sees the purpose of the variation as "to drive the point home."[92]

It would be unnecessary to argue that John sees the spiritual experience of each group as exclusively theirs. However, we do see some progression here, especially if we take the three categories of "children," "young men," and "fathers" as implying different stages in spiritual growth. For the children (*teknia/paidia*) there are both the experiences of forgiveness of sin ("your sins have been forgiven on account of his name," *apheōntai humin hai hamartiai dia to onoma autou*, 2:12b) and knowledge of the Father ("you have known the Father," *egnōkate ton patera*, 2:14a). The spiritual journey of the believer starts with forgiveness of sin. John had told his readers in 1:8 that a denial of having sin is a deception of self. A believer is one

---

89. See for example, Oepke 1967: 635–54; Moulton and Milligan 1930: 474 and 628; and Bauer, 1957: 609, 815.

90. Moulton and Milligan 1930: 628.

91. Jobes 2014: 102.

92. Lieu 2008: 86.

who has come to that point where he or she has said, "I am a sinner" and in faith "confessed sin" (1:9) and then received the blessings of Jesus being his or her *hilasmos* (propitiation, 2:2) or the means by which God now turns his face toward him or her as a Father. It brings a new experience of not just knowing that God exists out there somewhere but a relationship John describes as "knowledge of." It is deeper than knowledge about. It includes a personal experience of how this person is like.[93] This knowledge comes on account of Jesus' name. It is when we go before God and use the name of Jesus as the basis for God's acceptance of us that we get to know God in this way. This is because by ourselves alone we cannot stand before God who is light (1:5), but on account of Jesus who is righteous (2:1) we can begin this experiential knowledge with God. By implication, taking the meaning of *hoti* in these three verses as causal[94] (the reason why he writes), those he refers to as children are standing on a first step from which they can move on into the depths of the things he is writing. Their status[95] is one of a "forgiven people" and "living in experience with God as Father."

The second level is that of the young men (*neaniskoi*) though John mentions them last in both listings. Three things are said about them. They are overcomers ("you have overcome the evil one," *nenikēkate ton ponēron*, 2:13, 14), they are strong ("you are strong," *ischuroi este*, 2:14) and they are obedient ("the word of God remains in you," *ho logos tou theou en humin menei*, 2:14). John uses a perfect tense, *nenikēkate*, for their victory. The perfect is to be understood as intensive. They have attained the status of being

---

93. John uses *ginōskō* or its form twenty-five times in this epistle (2:3, 4, 5, 13, 13, 14, 18, 29; 3:1, 6, 16, 19, 20, 24; 4:2, 6, 7, 8, 13, 16; 5:2, 20). He also uses *oida* (2:11, 20, 21, 29; 3:2, 5, 14, 15; 5:13, 15, 18, 19, 20). Even if there are some of the usages of the two words here that may be debated, it seems clear that he uses *ginōskō* when the experience of the heart is in focus and *oida* when the knowledge of mind is in focus.

94. There is a minority view that sees the *hoti* here (2:12, 13, 14) as introducing dependent statements (declarative use, to be translated as "that"). See some discussion of this in Smalley 1984: 71; and Marshall 1978: 136–37. Haas et al. (1972: 55), for example, take this view but it does not make as much sense to say that John is passing information to his readers about these matters as it is that these matters are the bases on which he is able to write to them. John is not here saying that he has examined their souls with a telescope or observed their character and so would like to now tell them the marks they have scored. Rather, he is telling them that because they have attained these different things, he can now build on them to move them on to higher grounds.

95. Both perfect verbs, *apheōntai* (have been forgiven) and *egnōkate* (have known) are best taken as intensive. The focus is not so much on the action just as having happened but the result the action has produced. It is a privilege for the believer to know that he or she is a forgiven person and that God is his or her father.

victors. He uses a present tense, *este*, for their being strong. This is also their status, taking the present tense here as perfective. Its focus is the reality of past action. The more battles they have won, the more spiritual strength they have acquired. John can evaluate them and say "you are strong" and on that basis, I know I am not wasting time as I exhort you on the issues I am writing to you about. The present tense *menei* translated as "remains" can be taken as a durative present. As their general habit, they allow the word of God to control their lives. This has helped them to achieve what they are now (conquerors and strong) and forms a good basis for what John is writing to them about. The phrase "the word of God" (*ho logos*[96] *tou theou*) is making reference to the will of God as expressed in the Scriptures as his readers knew it. God has revealed it for the believer to be led by it. Jesus' victory over the evil one as recorded in Matt 4:1–11 and Luke 4:1–13 is a clear demonstration on the centrality of God's word in being conquerors. This is a clear reminder of the relationship between the place we give to the word of God and the victory we are able to attain. Paul in Eph 6:17 refers to the word of God (*rhema theou*) as the sword of the Spirit (*machaira tou pneumatos*). God has given or spoken the word (taking *theou* as genitive of source) and the Spirit uses the word (taking *pneumatos* as subjective genitive) to enable us to win the battle.

"Fathers" is the third level and John describes them twice but in the exact same way. They have known the one from the beginning ("you have known the one from the beginning," *egnōkate ton ap' archēs*, 2:13, 14). They have the experience of walking with him. Whether the one from the beginning is God the Father or God the Son makes no difference.[97] Knowledge of one is knowledge of the other (John 14:7–11).

Taking the three verses together we note that John writes to the "children" because:

1. Their sins have been forgiven on account of his name (2:12b)
2. They have known the Father (2:14a)

He writes to the "Fathers" because:

---

96. John uses the word *logos* six times in this epistle and apart from 1:1, which can be debated, the rest (1:10; 2:5, 7, 14; 3:18) have to do with word spoken rather than the technical usage of it in the Gospel of John (1:1) to refer to the person of Christ. When, therefore, it is described as "of God" it is equivalent to the Scriptures.

97. The commentaries, however, do show some differences of opinion. See discussion in Smalley 1984: 73–74.

The Ageless Commandment—Old Yet New (2:7–17)

1. They have known the one from the beginning (2:13a)
2. The same is repeated exactly in 2:14b

He writes to the "young men" because:

1. They have overcome the evil one (2:13b)
2. They are strong (2:14c)
3. The word of God remains in them (2:14c)
4. Exact repetition of no. 1 above, in 2:14c

Whether one views these classifications as referring to the same group of people from different perspectives or to three different groups, each of them has come to the level of believing in Jesus. By virtue of that experience, they are able to appreciate the command of love John writes to them in this section.

The fourth issue of using the present tense (*graphō*) in the first set (2:12–13) but the aorist tense (*egrapsa*) in the second set (2:14) also calls for comment. The literal translation of *graphō* is "I write" or "I am writing" and that of *egrapsa* is "I wrote." While the present tense, *graphō*, is clear John means this epistle (1 John), the aorist tense, *egrapsa*, can imply that John had written another epistle earlier, to these same readers.[98] This, however, is not necessary because it is not uncommon for a writer to write either within the perspective of where he/she sits as the writing is taking place or the perspective of the reader when he/she is reading the already written letter. This means that a writer can use "I write" and "I wrote" while referring to the same letter, depending on the glasses he/she has on at a given time. In the Greek language studies, this use of the aorist tense is referred to as "epistolary aorist"[99] and this is what we most likely have here (2:14). This is why the NIV, for example, uses "I write" in both sets of statements even though the Greek has two different tenses. This provision in the Greek

---

98. We are not aware of any earlier epistle John had written before 1 John. 2 John could be a possibility since it is addressed to "the chosen lady and her children" who could be a congregation (see comments under 2 John) but that would be a mere guess. Its content also, together with that of 1 John 1:1–2:13, which could also be the referent as John uses "I wrote" in 2:14, do not have the substance of what he states in 2:14 to have written. The epistolary use of the aorist tense seems to be the most reasonable explanation here.

99. Some other examples of a writer using aorist tense in view of wearing the glasses of the reader include *epempsa* (not *pempō*) in Acts 23:30, Eph 6:22, Phil 2:28, Col 4:8, Phlm 12, and *egrapsa* (not *graphō*) in Gal 6:11 and 1 John 2:21, among others.

language can be utilized simply for purpose of variation or emphasis. As Kruse says, the use of both present and aorist tenses here probably serves "as a stylic device to heighten the rhetorical effect of what he is writing."[100]

Love Toward the Father

John is not only interested in his believing readers exercising the horizontal love but also the vertical love. In fact, it is the vertical relationship (with God) that makes it possible to have harmonious relationship with other persons.

The love of the Father is expressed within the context of prohibition not to love things that would strangle the love of the Father. This calls to mind Jesus' words that one cannot serve two masters (Matt 6:24). John tells his readers, "Do not love the world nor the things in the world" (2:15, *mē agapate ton kosmon mēde ta en tō kosmō*). The prohibition here is expressed using *mē* and present imperative,[101] and this allows for the possibility that John's readers (at least some) were already at fault in this matter.[102] John, however, tells them that love for the world and the things in it (*kosmos* here understood as that system which is in opposition to the things of God[103]) excludes love of the Father. He says, "If anyone loves the world, the love of the Father is not in him" (*ean tis agapa ton kosmon, ouk estin hē agapē tou patros en autō*, 2:15b). The use of the third class condition here (projecting a possible situation, and not asserting a particular occurrence as a first class

---

100. Kruse 2000: 91.

101. The other way of expressing prohibition in Greek is by using *mē* with aorist subjunctive.

102. The distinction between the use of aorist subjunctive and present imperative for prohibitions, that the former prohibits an action not yet started while the present imperative prohibits an action already in progress, has been brought into question by some scholars (See, for example, Wallace 1996: 714–17). The suggested alternative, however, raises some questions. For example in reference to this particular passage, Kruse says, "The author is presenting the love of the world . . . as an ongoing action" (2000: 94). Does this mean a love of the world that is not ongoing is allowed? It would not make good sense. The context may be the more basic principle than an assumed rule.

103. The use of world (*kosmos*) in John is varied. Among other possible meanings, it is used to refer to the natural place of habitation (John 1:10a), the people who live in it (John 1:29; 3:16), and a system that is in opposition to the will of God (John 1:10b; 14:17). Such passages as John 1:10 and 3:17 seem to utilize more than one meaning of *kosmos* in the same verse.

The Ageless Commandment—Old Yet New (2:7-17)

condition would[104]) does not necessarily mean that the prohibition above cannot be an actual happening for some of his readers. He could here be stating the general principle that would apply to anyone if the condition is allowed so as to enforce the prohibition as it actually affected some. The genitive "of the Father" (*tou patros*) is here best taken as objective genitive. The one who loves the world is not able to love the Father also. There is a choice one must make for the two cannot go together. The reason for this exclusion is that what is in the world does not come from the Father (*ouk estin ek tou patros*). It is not his will. Specifically, what is in the world, in this negative usage, include, "lust of the flesh," "lust of the eyes," and "pride of life" (*hē epithumia tēs sarkos kai hē epithumia tōn ophthalmōn kai hē alazoneia tou biou*, 2:16)

The Greek word *epithumia* is neutral, with its context left to tell the reader whether it is negative or positive.[105] In this context (qualified by two genitives, "of the flesh" and "of the eyes") even as the translation provided communicates that it is negative. It is that strong desire that is driven by the flesh or/and the gluttony of the eyes,[106] rather than the will of God. It shows itself in such evil practices as satisfying the evil desires of the flesh and grabbing what is not ours. It does not ask what is acceptable by God and a blessing to my fellow human beings, but it always thinks of self. No wonder John adds the third element, "pride of life." Such a person places self above others and does not seek to submit to the will of God. It is a life characterized by pride.[107] It is interesting to note that Satan attempted to have Jesus fail in these three same areas. He targeted the desire of his flesh as he asked him to change stones into bread, the desire of his eyes as he showed him what he would give to him, and his attitude toward the will of God as he challenged him to throw himself down from the pinnacle of the temple (Matt 4:1-11 and Luke 4:1-13). Jesus demonstrated well that the choice is clear cut. One either stays within the will of God or entertains lust and pride. Choice of one excludes the other. This is the same point John is

---

104. A first class condition would have *ei* and the indicative mood. Here we have *ean* and the subjunctive mood.

105. Examples of its usage in a positive sense include Luke 22:15 and 1 Thess 2:17.

106. Both genitives *tēs sarkos* and *tōn ophthalmōn* can be taken as genitives of source. That is where the lust here originates from. The flesh and the eyes are the instruments used by Satan, the master of lust, to bring forth this lust.

107. The genitive *biou* as it qualifies "pride" is best taken as attributed or reverse genitive (cf. Wallace 1996: 89). Literal translation would be "proud life."

making here. It draws from what the first Adam (Rom 5:19a) failed in (Gen 3:6, 17), and the second Adam succeeded in (Rom 5:19b) as an example for us.

With the first reason for obeying the prohibition, "do not love the world" (*mē agapate ton kosmon*), being that such a love excludes love of the Father, John finishes this section with a second reason why obedience to the prohibition is important. In fact, it is the wiser thing to do. He says, in 2:17, "the world and its lust pass away, but the one who does the will of God remains forever" (*ho kosmos paragetai kai hē epithumia autou, ho de poiōn to thelēma tou theou menei eis ton aiōna*). The world provides opportunities for expression of lusts. Those who put their trust in those lusts, at the expense of loving God, end up miserable for what the world offers. However, the one who continues in the love of the Father lasts into eternity as the Father himself is eternal. This is very true in our life experiences. Accumulation of pleasure, wealth, and fame do not go with us when we die. We leave them all behind as we enter the next phase of life. In that next phase of life, it is those who have lived in obedience to God who continue to enjoy his fellowship as their Father. What a challenge in terms of how we view what we have or are! As Paul said, they are "rubbish" if they in any way come into competition with the place of Christ in our lives (Phil 3:7). At times, the experience of pursuing the world's promises and ending up being disappointed occurs within one's earthly life. Some have pursued earthly pleasures and ended with serious sicknesses, others have pursued wealth by wrong means and ended up in prison, and others have sought their satisfaction in fame later to commit suicide when the fame is there no more. The world promises but never delivers. If we may draw again from Satan's temptation of Jesus, were the things he promised in Matt 4:9 and Luke 4:6 truly his to give away? He created none of them.[108] He entices with lies, and only the unwise listen to him!

THE PRESENT ENEMY (2:18–27)

> (2:18) Children, it is the last hour, and just as you heard that an antichrist comes, even now many antichrists have come into being; by this we know that it is the last hour (19) From us they went

---

108. In Luke 4:6 Satan said, "It has been given to me" and even that cannot be trusted. God has never given over the governance of the universe to someone else. He may, at times, permit others to do their will but ultimately he remains the owner.

out, but they were not of us; for if they were of us, they would have remained with us; but in order that they may be exposed that all of them were of us (20) And you (yourselves) have an annointing from the holy one and know all (21) I do not write[109] to you because you do not know the truth but because you know it, and because no lie is of the truth (22) Who is the liar except the one who says that Jesus is not the Christ; this is the antichrist, the one who denies the Father and the Son (23) Everyone who denies the Son does not have the Father either; the one who confesses the Son has the Father also (24) What you (yourselves) heard from (the) beginning, let it remain in you; If what you heard from (the) beginning remains in you, you will also remain in the Son and in the Father (25) And this is the promise which he himself promised to us, life that is eternal (26) These things I write[110] to you concerning those leading you astray (27) And you, the annointing which you received from him remains in you and you have no need that anyone teaches you; but as his annointing teaches you concerning all, and is true and not a lie, and just as it taught you, remain in him.

Two very essential "legs" on basis of which any Christian community stands or falls are what it believes and what it practices. John has so far (1:1—2:17) focused on matters to do with practice, centering on the unchangeable truth that God is light (1:5) and how that applies in the exercise of love. This section brings in the second leg (belief) with the central issue being who Jesus is. While John's exhortation on matters of practice do not spell out a specific person or group who had misbehaved in a particular manner (the use of third class condition is to be noted) the section on belief spells out a group who had departed from the truth as to who Jesus is. John refers to the group as "they" as opposed to "we," qualified with the key statement *ex hēmōn exēlthan* (literally, "from us they went out") in 2:19. *Exēlthan* is in indicative mood, making a statement of fact.

There is no doubt that this is one of the clearest passages in 1 John as to what was happening at Ephesus when John wrote the epistle. Theologically, there were those who were denying that "Jesus is the Christ" (*Iesous estin ho Christos*, 2:22).[111] Such a position would have as its basis a view like that

---

109. This translates an aorist (*egrapsa*) but is rendered as a present because it is taken to be epistolary here.

110. Here we have another epistolary aorist.

111. From the context of 1 John, in which Jesus has been described as advocate and *hilasmos* (2:1-2) this statement is deeper than just declaring that Jesus is the Messiah. It is probably "a reference to the truth about the divine nature of Jesus Christ as both Messiah

Jesus was just a human being, different from what the same human being was later believed to be, that is, the Christ. Christ thus becomes a human-created object of faith. Relating it to our modern New Testament studies, it amounts to a denial of the fact that the Jesus of history (the person who walked the paths of Palestine) is the same one as the Christ of faith[112] (the one who the New Testament says is God's appointed way for redemption of humankind). Socially, the Ephesian church had become divided.[113] There were the secessionists who, as mentioned above, John describes as having gone out (*ex hēmōn*[114] *exēlthan*, 2:19).[115] For John, their departure was a proof that they did not belong, in the first place. In fact, for John, they are

---

and Son of God" (Jobes 2014: 130).

112. While the sophistication of expression during the time of John and our time may differ in degree, it amounts to the same thing—a separation of the humanity and deity of Christ. During the first and second centuries AD, it may have taken the form of Docetism (Christ only appeared to be a man, but he was not; the Greek verb *dokeō* meaning "I seem," "appear to be") or Ebionism (Jesus was a mere man and no more, only that he was appointed to be special during the time of his baptism).

113. By seeing a contrast between the "we" and "you" in this passage, Lieu argues that the addressee of John remained intact but the division (going out of us) was at the teachers' level, not at the believers' level. The believers John is writing to are just being warned so as to watch in case teachers who deny that Jesus is the Christ bring their teachings to them. Lieu says, "The repeated use of 'us' in contrast to the 'you' of the following verse (v. 20) suggests that the problem has arisen not in the community to whom the author is writing but among those whom he has only identified as 'we'" (2008: 101). See more on this in the introduction, under "historical context."

114. Keeping in mind that John is writing to his readers because he is not with them (a situation that would be so if he was writing to a local congregation), the "us" from where the false teachers went out from needs to be seen as the community of the faithful who adhered to the teachings of the apostles. The church is built on the teachings of Christ, especially his being the Christ (Matt 16:16–18) and the apostles' teaching is the foundation on which any teacher would build (Eph 2:20). A departure from that would qualify into "going out of the community of the faithful." There were some in John's time who had done this and so the basis of the concern here. These had the potential of influencing John's readers, and thus the firm statements of reminder as to who Jesus really is.

115. Keeping in mind that John is writing to his readers because he is not with them (a situation that would be so if he was writing to a local congregation), the "us" from where the false teachers went out from needs to be seen as the community of the faithful who adhered to the teachings of the apostles. The church is built on the teachings of Christ, especially his being the Christ (Matt 16:16–18) and the apostles' teaching is the foundation on which any teacher would build (Eph 2:20). A departure from that would qualify into "going out of the community of the faithful." There were some in John's time who had done this and so the basis of the concern here. These had the potential of influencing John's readers, and thus the firm statements of reminder as to who Jesus really is.

The Present Enemy (2:18–27)

antichrists (2:18). John labels them as antichrists[116] because the reason for their departure is denial that Jesus is the Christ, as John and those faithful to his teaching insisted. There is an implied pastoral lesson here: instead of large numbers in the midst of which are false teachers, departure of those who do not accept key fundamentals of faith may lessen the numbers, but eventually it is a blessing to a congregation. As a beginning point, their departure helps to show that they did not belong anyway. Those who belong persist in the truth, even when the winds against what the Scripture teaches seem very strong. Another blessing is that they take the leaven away with them instead of affecting others in close proximity. John refers to them, in 2:26, as "those leading you astray" (*tōn planōntōn humas*).[117] False teachers are never satisfied until they earn themselves a following.

For those who may have thought that they were doing kindness to the doctrine of God (monotheism) by denying that Jesus is the Christ, John in 2:23 tells them in plain words, "everyone who denies the Son does not have the Father, also" (*pas ho arnoumenos ton hyion oude ton patera echei*). It is safer to accept the mystery of the doctrine of Trinity than to solve the mystery by making the Son less being than the Father. Such a solution distances one from the Father, even when it is done to protect the truth that "God is one." In the one God are the Father and the Son (also, the Holy Spirit though he is not mentioned here for that was not the issue at Ephesus). It is this same error that we see in such groups as Jehovah's Witnesses of today.[118] In their guarding monotheism, they end up teaching that the Son was not the second person of the Trinity but the first creation of God (citing

---

116. The term *antichristos* (antichrist) is found only in the Epistles of John (1 John 2:18, 22; 4:3; and 2 John 7). The preposition *anti* can mean "instead of" or "against." It is the latter meaning that fits the context here. The secessionists were holding a position contrary to the truth John had taught them about Jesus being the Christ.

117. The act of "leading astray" does not need to be seen within the context of effected outcome (in either durative or iterative present senses) but the potential there is in view of the doubts the false teachers are planting. The shade of the present tense may best be taken here as tendential. John is writing to prevent an action the false teachers have not achieved yet but would love to achieve.

118. The teachings of Jehovah's witnesses stem from Arius (thus Arianism) of the fourth century AD. His motive was to protect the oneness of God, but in doing so he made Jesus less than God (presenting him as the first in God's creation) and the Holy Spirit less than a person (equating him with the impersonal power of God). It ends up as a heretical teaching even when its desire is admirable. We must admit mystery where there is one rather than simplify thoughts in a manner that distorts the teachings of Scripture and consequently mislead others.

Col 1:15 to support their position).[119] We must accept in humility the mystery of the Trinity—three Persons but one essence.

In contrast to the false teachers are the faithful, whom John refers to as "you" (*humeis, humin*, 2:20, 21, 24, 26, 27) and includes them in the "us" and "our" (2:19, 25). These faithful ones are to keep in mind that such a happening is part of prophecy. It is the last hour and one of the things concerning that hour is that "an antichrist comes" (*antichristos erchetai*[120]) and this is already a reality for "many antichrists have come into being" (*antichristoi polloi*[121] *gegonasin*).

Bearing in mind that the time they live in is the last hour,[122] what they need to do is remain in what is the truth. In 2:24 they are told, "what

---

119. Of special interest, in this passage, to Jehovah's witnesses is the description of Christ as *prōtotokos pasēs ktiseōs* rendered "firstborn over all creation" in NKJB, HCSB, NIV, and others. Rather than mean "first" in the order in which creation took place, the word *prōtotokos* means first in terms of majesty. This is the idea the translations are capturing with the use of "over" all creation. The literal translation of the entire Greek phrase is "first-born of all creation" (see NASB). When the genitive *pasēs ktiseōs* ("of all creation") is taken as objective, the idea is "the ruler who governs all creation." This agrees well with the entire passage (Col 1:15–20). The focus is the prominence of Christ and not his origin.

120. A futuristic present (a future happening but so certain that present tense is used to express it) is used here to emphasize the certainty of the coming of an antichrist. While it is only John who uses this title (see note 115 above) the same phenomenon is described in Paul, using the term "man of lawlessness" (2 Thess 2:3) and the Synoptics using "false Christs" or "false prophets" (Matt 24:4–5, 11, 24; and Mark 13:22). See a comparative study of the same in Kruse 2000: 99–100.

121. Many (*polloi*) is a relative term, and can mean any number from two to millions. Within the context here, they are not the single one (antichrist) but they prefigure him, teaching what characterizes his doctrine. When it comes to false teaching, even "two false teachers" are two too many. False teaching is very contentious.

122. Though the exact phrase (last hour, *eschatē hōra*) is found only here in the New Testament, it is the same period of time referred to as "last days" (2 Tim 3:1; Heb 1:2; Jas 5:3; 2 Pet 3:3) or last times (1 Pet 1:20). The phrase "invokes the eschatological concept of the final stage of God's dealings with the world, a stage inaugurated with the death of Jesus, extending through a period of world's hostility toward followers of Christ, and to be consummated on the day of resurrection and judgment at the end of history as we know it" (Jobes 2014: 123). Ngewa says that this period covers "the entire period from Pentecost until Christ returns, which is the next major event in God's plan for the world" (2009: 87). The phrase can be used for any part of this period, depending on what the focus is.

The Present Enemy (2:18–27)

you heard[123] from the beginning,[124] let it remain[125] in you" (*ho ēkousate ap' archēs, en humin menetō*) and in 2:27: "just as it[126] taught[127] you, remain in him"[128] (*kathos edidaxen humas, menete en autō*). John assures them that by remaining in what they have been taught, they remain "in the Son and in the Father" (*en tō huiō kai en tō patri*). John defines this fellowship (abiding in) with the Son and Father as "eternal life" (*tēn zōēn tēn aiōnion*) and qualifies it as promise (2:25) God has made.[129] John's readers just needed to reflect on this truth and on that basis ignore anyone who desired to lead them astray. A relationship guaranteed by God's promise cannot change.

---

123. Within the immediate context, what the readers heard is that Jesus is the Christ, but it does not need to be limited to it. It has the implications, among others, of walking as he walked and refusing all idols (5:21) that could make the readers unfaithful to him.

124. The beginning here is best taken as when they came to faith. That marked the beginning of their spiritual experience.

125. A present tense is used here. It is not one-time determination but life-long goal. The truth taught to them is to be their theological position and way of life at all times, and in all circumstances.

126. The identity of "it" here is "the anointing" (*chrisma*, 2:26, 27). It is presented, in 2:27, as both having taught them in the past (*edidaxen*) and also teaching them now (*didaskei*). It makes good sense to see this as a reference to the ministry of the Holy Spirit in light of John 14:26. John's use of the term for the ministry of the Holy Spirit may have been influenced by the false teachers' possible use of *chrisma* as the means by which they, according to their claim, received special revelation beyond what they had been taught (Kruse 2000: 108; Jobes 2014: 132). An alternative position is to see *chrisma* as making reference to some kind of ritual (like baptism) that we cannot identify specifically (Lieu 2008: 103). This, however, may have difficulties in explaining that the *chrisma* taught and even teaches the readers.

127. In terms of the content of the teaching, John uses the phrase *peri pantōn* (concerning all things) and as to its nature says, *alēthes estin kai ouk estin pseudos* (it is true and it is not a lie). Specifically, it is who Jesus is but in general it includes all things they have been taught by him. He is the Spirit of truth (4:6; 5:6).

128. The role of the third person of the Trinity is very prominent here. He is the source of the anointing (2:27a, *autou* in both *ap' autou* and *to autou chrisma* can be taken as genitive of source) and he is the object the readers are called for continued relationship with (2:27b). Whatever lessons he teaches concerning Jesus, it is not only true but also from the highest authority on the subject. When someone has received instructions from the highest authority on a matter, he/she does not need instructions from a less authority, and much more so when the instructions from the less authority contradicts the teachings of the highest one.

129. This is a clear statement that the focus of the term "eternal life" is not duration but relationship with God. The duration is the product of the relationship, for God is eternal.

John was clear that the privilege of being taught is not just a past event. The annointing (*chrisma* 2:20, 26, 27) remains[130] in them (*menei en humin*) and teaches them (*didaskei*, 2:27) even now. With such a teacher they need no other person to teach them ("you do not have need that anyone teaches you," *ou chreian echete hina tis didaskē humas*). It is a privilege to have the best of teachers and when one has that privilege, there is no need of looking for another.[131]

John assures his readers that he is writing to them, not because they are ignorant of the truth but because they know it (2:21). In other words, he is not writing to inform, but to exhort or establish. The fact that Jesus is the Christ is not a new thought. It is something they know and just need to be reminded of the importance of holding on to it in the midst of the false teaching around them. Whatever deviates from what they know already, which is the truth, is a lie (2:21). There is always a blessing in hearing God's word again and again. We may know all that is in Gen 1:1 to Rev 22:21 but we still need to hear it again and again, and in a fresh way. It addresses our changing circumstances and needs in a different way every time we hear it. Those who boast of when they began going to church, for the purpose of showing that they do not need to be taught anything by the evangelists or pastors, miss the point that God's word is fresh every time we hear it in sincerity of heart.

Our Status and Obligation as Children of God (2:28–3:10)

> (2:28) And now, children, remain in him, so that when he is revealed[132] you may have boldness and not be ashamed from him at his coming (29) if you know (*eidēte*) that he is righteous, you also know (*ginōskete*) that everyone who does righteousness has been

---

130. The chain of remaining here is worth noting. The *chrisma* remains in them (2:27), they let what they were taught remain in them (2:24a), and they remain in the Son and the Father (2:24b). The first is a statement of reality, the second is an exhortation/command, and the last is the outcome. God's blessings are dependent on obedience and obedience is made possible by God's provision.

131. Passages like this one (see also John 14:26) have been used by some to dismiss the need for Bible training. That, however, is wrong understanding of what John is teaching. His point is that the Holy Spirit is the teacher of truth and anyone who teaches contrary to his teachings must be ignored. As we have it now, the Holy Spirit's teaching is found in the Scriptures. Going for Bible training to learn the Scriptures is in line with the Holy Spirit teaching us.

132. This translates an aorist tense, which is understood to be a proleptic aorist.

Status and Obligation as Children of God (2:28–3:10)

born of him (3:1) See what manner of of love the Father has given to us, that we have been called[133] children of God, and we are. On account of this the world does not know (*ginōskei*) us, because it did not know (*egnō*) him (2) Beloved, we are now children of God, and it has not yet been revealed[134] what we shall be. We know (*oidamen*) that when he is revealed, we will be like him, because we shall see him just as he is (3) And everyone who has this hope in him purifies himself, just as he himself is pure (4) Everyone who does sin does lawlessness also, sin is also lawlessness (5) and you know (*oidate*) that he was revealed, in order that he might take away sins, and there is no sin in him (6) Everyone who remains in him does not sin (as a practice). Everyone who sins (as a practice) has neither seen him nor known (*egnōken*) him (7) Children, let no one deceive you; the one who practices righteousness is righteous, just as he (himself) is righteous (8) The one who practices sin is of the devil, because the devil practices sin from the beginning. For this purpose the Son of God was revealed, that he might destroy the works of the devil (9) Everyone who has been born of God does not do sin as normal practice, because his (God's) seed remains in him, and he is not able to sin as a practice, because he has been born of God (10) In this the children of God are made clear and the children of the devil: everyone who does not do righteousness is not of God, and everyone who does not love his brother.

With the earlier section (2:18-27) having focused on what to watch out (false teaching), John in this section reminds his readers what to keep on growing in—the obligation that comes with their status as children of God.

Using the endearment title *tekna* ("children") twice here (the vocative form is used in 2:28 and 3:7) and also the title *agapētoi* ("beloved ones," used in 3:2) John reminds his readers of their status, namely, they are children of God. Three times he makes the assertion and three times implies it. In 3:1 he says, "we have been called children of God, and we are" (*tekna theou*[135] *klērōmen, kai esmen*); in 3:2, "we are now children of God" (*nyn*

---

133. This translates an aorist, given here a resultative shade, and thus the translation as a perfect.

134. This also translates an aorist, judged here to be a resultative aorist.

135. The genitive *theou* ("of God") here, and also in 3:2 and 3:10, is a genitive of relationship. God relates to the believers as his children. In human relationships, the one to whom one is a child underlines his/her status. To have God as father is the highest status one can have. John emphasizes this status by the use of "we are." The present tense

tekna theou esmen); and in 3:10, "in/by this the children of God are made clear" (*en toutō phanera estin ta tekna tou theou*). He makes the same statement implicitly as he uses the metaphor of being born of God thrice: 2:28, "has been born[136] of him" (*ex autou gegennētai*); 3:9a, "everyone who has been born of God" (*pas ho gegennēmenos ek tou theou*) and 3:9b, "because he/she has been born of God" (*hoti ek tou theou gegennētai*).

John contrasts the status of being children of God to that of being of the devil. In 3:8 he says "he/she is of the devil" (*ek tou diabolou estin*) and in 3:10 refers to those who sin as *ta tekna tou diabolou*[137] ("the children of the devil"). As 3:10 clearly shows, the differentiating marks are one's response to God's righteousness since God is light (1:5: *ho theos phōs estin*) and righteous (2:28: *dikaios estin*), and relationship with fellow human beings because God is love (4:8: *ho theos agapē estin*[138]) and expects his children to also love each other.

John spells out three things as the bases of both the status and state of being children of God. These are (1) the love of God, "see what manner of love the Father has given to us" (3:1: *idete potapēn agapēn dedōken hēmin ho patēr*); (2) the revelation of the Son of God, "you know that he was revealed so that he might take away sins" (3:5: *oidate hoti ekeinos ephanerōthē, hina tas hamartias arē*) and "for this purpose the Son of God was revealed, that he might destroy the works of the devil" (3:8b: *eis touto ephanerōthē ho hyios tou theou, hina lusē ta erga tou diabolou*[139]); and (3) abiding presence of the Holy Spirit, "his seed remains in him" (3:9: *sperma autou en autō menei*). Admittedly, the identification of *sperma autou* ("his seed") that John

---

esmen (we are) is progressive/durative. It is our status without a break. At times, we may feel like this is not the case, but our status is not based on how we feel but what God has declared. It is a relationship that causes us to be at peace at all times.

136. It is the act of "being born of God" that gives a believer the status of being a child of God (see note 134 above). It is an expression meant to describe when the status of being God's child begins. Its realization is by receiving Jesus as one's Savior (John 1:12).

137. This genitive "of the devil" (*tou diabolou*) is also genitive of relationship. The description has in mind the person who conducts his/her life with the devil as master.

138. The verb "is" (*estin*) in all the three verses is a gnomic present. The nature of God is light, righteous, and love at all times. That is his character.

139. The genitive "of the devil" (*tou diabolou*) is subjective genitive. It is the works the devil generates that Christ came to destroy. He generated these works in the Garden of Eden (in the case of Adam and Eve) and also generates these works in the descendants of Adam and Eve (which we all are) by deceiving us to live in disobedience to God.

Status and Obligation as Children of God (2:28–3:10)

says remains in the one who has been born of God is not clear. Identification of this seed as the Holy Spirit is only one of the possible views.[140]

The implications of this status include (1) purity of life, (2) love for others, and (3) distance from the world.

In 3:3, John says, "everyone who has this hope in him purifies himself" (*pas ho echōn tēn elpida tautēn ep' autō hagnizei heauton*). The hope here is that of full glorification, as John introduces it with the words, "when he is revealed[141] we shall be like him, because we will see him just as he is"[142] (3:2b: *ean phanerōthē, homoioi autō esometha, hoti opsometha auton kathōs estin*). The anticipation of greater glory becomes motivation for cultivating and maintaining the present degree of holiness. In this connection,

---

140. A basic question that needs to be answered is the shade (function/aspect) of the genitive pronoun "his" (in *sperma autou*). Is it a qualitative genitive or is it a genitive of source. If it is the latter, then identification of "*sperma*" here as Holy Spirit (see for example, Brown 1982: 411; Schnackenburg 1992: 175; Kruse 2000: 125; Burdick 1985: 247; Plummer 1888: 79; Burge 1996: 149) or God's word, that is, the gospel (see for example, Painter 2003: 229; Grayston 1984: 107) are viable interpretations. If we have here a qualitative genitive, then the identification needs to be understood in a more general sense of divine nature (see for example, Hobbs 1983: 88; Houlden 1973: 96; Lieu 1991: 35; Culy 2004: 77; Kysar 1986: 81; Smalley 1984: 172; and Westcott 1892: 107) comparable to the DNA a child would share with his/her parents. There are some (for example, Yarbrough 2008: 195) whose interpretation would amount to taking the genitive *autou* as possession or relationship (with the idea that God's seed [that is, his offspring] abides in him [God]) but that seems less likely within the flow of the argument in this context. Though the idea of the believer abiding is mentioned in 3:6, the focus in 3:9 seems to be more on the gracious provision of God to enable the believer not to sin than the believer hanging unto God.

141. John here talks of both the First and the Second Coming of Christ using the word "revealed" (*phanerōthē*). We find it in 2:28 (*ean phanerōthē*, when he is revealed), 3:2 (*oupō ephanerōthē*, not yet revealed), 3:2 (*ean phanerōthē*, when he is revealed), 3:5 (*ekeinos ephanerōthē*, he was revealed), and 3:8 (*eis touto ephanerōthē*, for this purpose he was revealed). The First Coming is expressed using the aorist indicative (*ephanerōthē*, 3:5, 8) and the Second Coming using the aorist subjunctive (*phanerōthē*, with *ean*, 2:28; 3:2). The First Coming is a fact of history. In his Gospel, John had expressed this by saying that the Word became flesh (John 1:14). The Second Coming also must be expected to take place as a matter of "fact in history." The use of subjunctive in reference to it is not whether it will happen or not but when it may happen. That is where the uncertainty is. It is a certain event whose scheduling depends on God and not on man. The requirement on our part is to conduct our lives as if it can happen any moment. God, in his perfect wisdom, kept this detail from us so that we can live in readiness at all times.

142. The current state of Christ is that of glory. He is eternally glorious; for a time he set aside his glory so as to accomplish the work of redemption on the cross; he ascended in glory and sits at the right hand of the Father (Acts 7:56; Col 3:1; Heb 1:3).

John makes several key statements about the believer and act of sinning. In 3:6 he says, "everyone who remains in him does not sin" (*pas ho en autō menōn ouch hamartanei*) and in 3:9, "everyone born of God does not do sin" (*pas ho gegennēmenos ek tou theou hamartian ou poiei*) and then adds that such a person "is not able to sin, because he/she has been born of God" (*ou dunatai hamartanein, hoti ek tou theou gegennētai*). As the translation provided above reflects, the present tenses here (*poiei, hamartanei,* and *dunatai hamartanein*) are best taken as durative present, focusing on the act of sinning as a habit. The one who has been born of God is given a nature, through which the Holy Spirit works, and as such would not permit continual practice of sin.[143] Until glorification, however, he or she can do an act of sin, which definitely leads to deep regret for not keeping the nature that conforms to the family of God.

---

143. While there are many others who agree that John's point here is that one who is born of God does not and cannot sin as a habit (see, for example, Stott 1964: 135; Kruse 2000: 120, 125; Grayston 1984: 105; Painter 2003: 230–31; Burge 1996: 149–50; Baugh 1999: 52; and Hobbs 1983: 85, 88) there are also competing views. Some of the key ones are that John is here to be understood as teaching that (1) the new (divine) nature does not and cannot sin (Plummer 1888: 79); (2) the ideal for being born of God is the impossibility of sinning though this may not be the reality (Westcott 1892: 90, 92); (3) one born of God does not and cannot commit willful or deliberate sin (Yarbrough 2008: 95); (4) sin is here to be understood as unbelief (Kysar 1986: 81) and so automatically excluding a believer; (5) sin is here to be understood as defined in 3:4, that is lawlessness (*anomia*), and seen as an act that is accompanied by refusal to confess and submit to God's authority (Jobes 2014: 48). The view that it is habitual or persistent sin that John has in mind here has been adopted, and with the following observation. The person has been born of God (perfect tense) and remains in Him (present tense). Is this remaining a guaranteed state or is it something the believer is to work on? Based on the use of the imperative in 2:28 (*menete*, keep on remaining), it appears as if the believer has a role to play in maintaining this state. What if the believer does not work on it? What we have here can be illustrated using a machine. It is manufactured to do a particular function (cf. we have been born of God to live a particular kind of life—a life of holiness and love). There are times, however, when the machine is out of order. What is required then is to repair the machine. It never ceases to be the machine it is—no matter to what extend it is out of order. Machines can be thrown away for they cannot be repaired any more, but there is no time when God cannot repair the believer back to what He purposed him or her to be. This is where God's patience comes into the picture even in the case where a believer has gone on in sin for a long time. So, what does it mean that one who is born of God cannot continue sinning? It means that there will be an arrest of the situation in one way or another. On the part of man, it is to return to God for repair. On the part of God, he may call such a person home. This may be what John has in mind when he talks of sin unto death and sin not unto death in 5:16. More comments on this are found under 5:16 below.

Status and Obligation as Children of God (2:28–3:10)

One aspect of the child of God purifying himself or herself is in the exercise of love. Without leaving out the matter of God's love toward us (for example, 4:9–11, 19) or our love for God (for example, 5:1–3) John focuses on our love for one another (the horizontal relationships). In this particular passage he lists love of the brother as one of the pointers of being a child of God as he says, "everyone who does not do righteousness is not of God, and the one who does not love his brother" (3:10b: *pas ho mē poiōn dikaiosunēn ouk estin ek tou theou, kai ho mē agapōn ton adelphon autou*). By implication, the one who does not love his or her brother or sister is *ek tou diabolou* ("of the devil"). John does not spare words in communicating that there are two families, spiritually. There is the family of God where the practice of love is a central matter in their constitution and there is the family of the devil to which those who do not love belong. The love in question here is not one that chooses who to love and leaves out some. It is a love that is sacrificial and makes no discrimination. It is patterned after God's own love who allows his enemies to keep on breathing the air he created. The use of the present tense *agapōn* is also important here. The exercise of this kind of love is the believer's continual practice. It is the way of life for the children of God. Obedience to it results in being right before God as judge.

The two contrasting worlds (of God and of Satan) and the two contrasting set of children (children of God and children of the devil) result in the world's (used here as the sphere the devil reigns) attitude toward the children of God. John tells his readers that on the basis of their being children of God "the world does not know us" (3:1a: *ho kosmos ou ginōskei*[144] *hēmas*). He adds that this should not be a surprise to them "because it did not know[145] him" (*hoti ouk egnō auton*). The pronoun "him" here refers to the Lord Jesus Christ. John in his Gospel says that he came to his own but his own did not receive him (John 1:11). They did not acknowledge him as the Messiah and in spite of all his teachings and acts of mercy before their

---

144. The act of "not knowing" here may be understood as a gnomic (customary) present. The child of God is from a family that the world is not familiar with, and consequently would not know the believer. It can also be taken as durative present and understand "knowing" in the sense of treating with some regard. The world has no place for the believer. It sees the believer as a misfit as the believer is from another sphere altogether. The durative present idea seems to go well with the fact that what the world does with the believer has precedence in what it did with the believer's master.

145. The aorist tense *egnōn* here is constative. In its dealing with Jesus, the world never understood who he was. This is seen from the point of his birth (born in a manger) all the way to his death (crucified like a criminal). In between, there was failure to recognize that he is the Messiah.

very eyes, they chose that a criminal be freed and Christ be crucified (John 18:39–40). Those who are children of God should, therefore, not expect any different treatment from the world. The children of God are to be distant to those of the devil in terms of refusal to be part of their ethical system while at the same time loving them as their heavenly Father loves all. This is a balance a number of believers find difficult to maintain, but it is the expected way of life in the family of God. The statement made by some, "if you love me, then you must be able to do this or that for me" (regardless of the necessary ethical considerations) must be screened by the believer through God's scanner. God loves all but hates every form of sin. So we also, as children of God, should hate whatever belongs to the sphere of the devil even as we love everyone.

In addition to our being motived by the past (God loved us and sent his Son) and the present (we are children of God), there is also a future dimension to this motivation. It should be our desire and prayer that we remain in him "so that when he is revealed we may have boldness and not be ashamed from[146] him at his coming" (2:28: *hina ean phanerōthē schōmen parrēsian*[147] *kai mē aischynthōmen ap' autou en tē parousia autou*). The future also holds a promise for us (3:2). John says, "we shall be like him" (*homoioi autō esometha*), that is, glorious.[148]

---

146. While it is attractive to render the expression *ap' autou* as "before him" (see NIV, NKJB), rendering it literally as "from him" is not altogether impossible. It is true that being "ashamed before him" paints a clearer picture here on basis of context. However, "being ashamed from him" can also make some sense if the idea is that they cannot face him. Their shame will lead them away from him. Drawing from what happens with a child who is conscious of an act of disobedience, rather than running toward an approaching parent the child will tend to stay away in fear. Confidence leads us toward our master while shame leads us away from the master. This is what Adam and Eve did. At the coming of their Creator, they hid themselves in shame and fear (Gen 3:8–10).

147. The Greek word *parresia* has the idea of confidence. It can also be illustrated from a child who is not conscious of any act of disobedience as she/he approaches a parent. It is an attitude of full confidence. When, however, a child is conscious of an act of disobedience, there is lack of confidence or courage as the child goes before a parent. The same can also be illustrated by confidence we all have when we are accused of something we know for certain we are not guilty of. There is an assurance that we face the situation with. The word is used four times in this epistle, with reference to confidence at the Lord's return (here and 4:17) and to approaching God in prayer (3:21 and 5:14).

148. What one aims at within the education context, whether it is an A grade or first class honors, becomes a motivator of how much effort one puts in the studies. While in this context the goal is not based on one's effort but a promise of God, it is not an average grade that is aimed at. It is the highest level one can achieve in matters of likeness to Christ. It is a sharing with him of his glory. With that as the focus, the level of moral

Love as a Characteristic of a Believer (3:11–18)

There is great joy on the part of a servant knowing that when the master comes he or she will be pleased. This gives confidence to the servant even as the master returns. We are not servants but children. We are the family of God. Our desire that our Lord and Savior will be pleased when he returns should be greater than that of a servant. After all, it is not only that we will have boldness and confidence as we meet him, but also we will inherit glorious body as he has. There is every reason for us to do our best to keep our present conduct pleasing to him.

Love, a Distinctive Characteristic of a Believer (3:11–18)

> (3:11) Because this is the message which you heard from (the) beginning, that we should love one another, (12) not as Cain (who) was of the devil and he slaughtered his brother; and for what did he slaughter him? Because his works were evil and his brother's were righteous (13) [and] do not marvel, brothers, if the world hates you (14) We (ourselves) know that we have passed from death into life, because we love the brothers. The one who does not love remains in death (15) everyone who hates his brother is a murderer, and you know (*oidate*) that no murderer has eternal life abiding in him. (16) In/by this we know (*egnōkamen*) (the) love, (in) that he gave his life (soul) for us; we (ourselves) also ought to give our lives (souls) for the brothers (17) whoever has the things of life of the world (material things) and happens to see his brother having need and closes the bowels of mercy from him (is not moved to help), how does the love of God remain in him? (18) Children, let us not love in word or with the tongue (only) but by deeds (works) and in truth.

John ends the previous section by spelling out two things that mark out who a child of God is. The two are "doing righteousness" and "loving a brother or sister" (3:10). Now, he expands the theme of love, not as a new message but as a message his readers have heard *ap' archēs* ("from the beginning"). This is most likely, the beginning of their spiritual experience as the subject of love is one that is very close to the heart of John.[149] It is not

---

purity, as children of God, becomes serious business.

149. In 1 John alone, John uses the word "love" in the verb form (*agapein*) twenty-four times, and as a noun (*agapē*) eighteen times. The same interest is also found in the Gospel, with the verb used thirty-five times and the noun six times. Compare this, for example, with Paul in whose thirteen epistles, the verb is found thirty-four times and the noun seventy-five times. Peter, in his two epistles, uses the verb only five times and the

surprising, therefore, that this is a second passage on the theme, and there will also be a third one (see comments under 4:7–21). The passage here may be examined using the outline (a) the commandment of love (b) examples about love—negative and positive, and (c) the practice of love.

The Commandment of Love

The content of the message John's readers have heard from the beginning is that "we should love one another" (3:11: *agapōmen allēlous*). The act of loving here is expressed in the present tense, which means this will be our habit. We do not love today and withhold love tomorrow. We must love all the time. The implication of this message to our world today is that there would be no fights among God's people and by extension in the societies the believers have influence on. The evidence in the public domain, however, is that fights among believers are more frequent than not, and this sets a negative example to others with the results that wars are a common feature of our everyday lives. It was a message for John's readers in the first century and as a relevant message for us today as then.

Examples of Love—Negative and Positive

In order not to leave the exhortation unclear to anyone, John brings into the picture two examples: one who lacked love to a very high degree, and the other, the ultimate example of love. The first took the life of another, and without cause, while the second gave his life for others.

Concerning the one who took the life of another, John says "not as Cain who was of the evil one and slew his brother" (3:12a: *ou kathōs Kain ek tou ponērou ēn kai esphaxen ton adelphon autou*). The word used for Cain's action here (*esphaxen*) is equivalent to "slaughtering."[150] John emphasizes the evil of this act by pointing out that Cain slew *ton adelphon autou* ("his brother"). While slaughtering without mercy is bad in every situation, it is much more so when it goes against the common saying that "blood is thicker than water." The natural expectation would be for a brother to defend a brother and not to kill a brother. Yet, the attitude Cain showed here

---

noun four times.

150. Though it is mostly found in the New Testament, in its noun form (*sphagē*—Acts 8:32; Rom 8:36; Jas 5:5) or participle form (Rev 5:6, 12; 6:9; 13:8; 18:24) the contexts make it clear that it has the connotation of violent murder. It is an outward expression of deep-seated hatred of the person or what he/she stands for.

seems to resemble what we witness in many parts of the world where we have war torn nations. Instead of a nation uniting to defend itself against an enemy from without, a fellow-citizen rises up to kill his or her fellow-citizen. Further still, instead of the human race uniting to fight common enemies like diseases, we fight each other mercilessly and spend billions of dollars financing wars. We thank God that those of us who are Jesus' followers have redefined our brother or sister to include all those with whom we relate to in Christ no matter their tribe or race.[151] In the same vein, we have come to view all beings as God views them, since we are his children. As we see every human being as God's creation in his image, any form of hatred, leave alone murder, becomes out of place in our daily practice. God fobid that the world continues to see multiplication of Cains!

John adds the reason why Cain slew his brother, Abel, to further stress the evil here. He asks, "and why [on what account] did he slaughter him?" (*kai charin tinos esphaxen auton*), to which he supplies the answer "because his works were evil but the ones of his brother were righteous" (3:12b: *hoti ta erga autou ponēra ēn ta de tou adelphou autou dikaia*). It was totally a matter of envy. Abel did no offense to Cain, and so even in the judgment of common sense, Cain had no reason for hurting Abel. It is no wander that John includes the phrase that Cain *ek tou ponērou* ("was of the evil one"). The devil creates enmity where there is no cause for it, for he loves fights and wars and murder. He hates it when there is love among brothers and looks for every opportunity to create tension among the best of friends. He is at work to destroy marriages, families, churches, institutions, and even nations. He plants Cain wherever he is given an opportunity. It is no surprise that Peter concluded his first epistle by exhorting his readers to resist him (1 Pet 5:9). He is an enemy to anything that is going well, based on acts of love for one another.

On the basis of this business of Satan, exemplified by Cain, John tells his readers, "do not marvel, brothers, if the world hates you" (3:13: *mē thaumazete,*[152] *adelphoi, ei misei humas ho kosmos*). The world here stands

---

151. This is not meant to say that every believer in Christ lives up to this standard. There are many who have failed or are failing. Their constitution (the Bible), however, condemns their deeds.

152. John expresses this prohibition using *mē* and a present imperative (*thaumazete*). Though it is questioned by some (for example, Wallace 1996: 714–17; also see note 102 above) it is still the understanding of many (including the writer here) that use of *mē* and present imperative expresses a prohibition of something that is already a reality, though subject to context. John was aware that the believers were wondering why those

for the systems within which the devil has been allowed to be in charge. God's permissive will allows the devil to appear to be in control of things until the appointed time when he will be thrown into the lake of fire (Rev 20:10). We also, at times (even as God's people), allow him to be in charge by choosing to obey him rather than obey God. The whole system within which Satan has been given a foothold fights against God and those who are in fellowship with him. John's *adephoi* (brothers), which includes all of us who are believers, should expect hatred of Satan and his system. To expect otherwise would be a failure to understand the dynamics at play. The world will (the condition *ei misei humas ho kosmos* is first class condition) hate the believer, not once but as a general practice.[153] Our neighbors, for example, may love to rob the widows and orphans and when we speak against it, we become their enemies. When we speak against greedy leaders we become targets for elimination. John says that this is what we should expect. Satan and his system hate truth and justice and peace. May the Lord help us to see matters in this perspective when we suffer for the sake of righteousness and never give up!

One can quickly respond to John's use of Cain as example and say, "I have murdered no one." John, however, points out that hatred alone amounts to murder. He says, "everyone who hates his brother is a murderer" (3:15a: *pas ho misōn ton adelphon autou anthrōpoktonos estin*). It is significant that John uses present tense (*misōn*) for the act of hating here. There is going to be a natural feeling of hatred toward those who mistreat us for no good cause. We must, however, quickly turn our feelings to love and stop the feeling of hatred. The one who hates a brother as a matter of practice belongs to the same category as one who takes another person's life. We are called to wish others well and not evil, prosperity and not calamity, salvation and not condemnation. It is not easy, but John says it is the expectation of God to whom we are children.

Within this context, John divides us into two categories: those in death and those in life. Those who abide in the sphere where Satan reigns are under death and their destiny is eternal condemnation. Those who

---

whose lives were like those of Abel (doing what was good) were experiencing hatred and even some degree of persecution. He wants his readers to know that there is this tension between good and evil. Without any justified cause, the evil system hates those who promote good.

153. The act of hating is expressed using the present tense, *misei*. It is the nature of the world, as a system under the control of the evil one, to hate what is good. The believer stands for the good and automatically becomes object of hatred.

Love as a Characteristic of a Believer (3:11–18)

obey God, however, enjoy fellowship with him and their ultimate end is eternal life. The very act of loving or hating marks who we are in terms of our eternal destiny. John says, "we know that we have crossed over from death into life, because we love the brothers" (3:14a: *hēmeis*[154] *oidamen hoti metabebēkamen*[155] *ek tou thanatou*[156] *eis tēn zōēn,*[157] *hoti agapōmen*[158] *tous adelphous*). To this John adds, "the one who does not love abides [remains] in death" (3:14b: *ho mē agapōn menei en tō thanatō*) and "you know that no murderer has eternal life abiding in him" (3:15b: *oidate hoti pas anthrōpoktonos ouk echei zōēn aiōnion en autō menousan*). There cannot be clearer stress on the need to love one another than we find here as God's people. Hatred, no matter what reasons we may give to justify our actions, is out of order. To love to hate is to confirm that we are a people of "death" and not a people of "life."

After telling his readers that hatred does not belong to God's children, he draws their attention to the ultimate example of love and then exhorts them on a practical way in which they will demonstrate this love toward each other.

Concerning the ultimate example, John says, "by this we know[159] love, that he gave his life for us" (3:16a: *en toutō egnōkamen tēn agapēn, hoti ekeinos huper hēmōn tēn psuchēn autou ethēken*). The "he" (*ekeinos*, literally "that one") here is Jesus Christ, our Savior and Lord. He died on the cross, so that by that act we may have life eternal.

---

154. We here have an emphatic first personal plural, "we ourselves..."

155. The perfect tense here is intensive. This is our status. We have crossed over, and no longer belong to the sphere of death.

156. This is a genitive of exit. We belonged to the sphere of death, but we have come out of it.

157. Here we have an adverbial accusative of termination. We have landed into the sphere of life. That is where we now belong.

158. This is a conditional use of the indicative and can even be translated as "if we love." It underlines how important the act of loving is, to John. It is also presented using a present tense. It is the way of life, of loving, that John has in mind here.

159. This (we know) translates a perfect tense, but the perfect tense here is best taken as focusing on our current state (intensive perfect). We are a people who are informed about this matter. The example of Christ, as to what it means to love, is before us as a vivid lesson.

The Practice of Love

On the basis of Christ's example, John exhorts, "we also ought to lay down the [our] lives for the brothers" (3:16b: *kai hēmeis opheilomen huper tōn adephōn tas psuchas theinai*). The love in question here is one that calls for sacrifice on the part of its giver for the benefit of the recipient. It is a total contrast to the example of Cain, who instead of sacrificing his own life to save his brother Abel, chose to take Abel's life. We are called to follow the example of Jesus.

The manner in which we will give our lives for others may be defined differently in differing circumstances. John, however, uses the example of our attitude toward our possessions when there is a call for us to respond to our brothers' or sisters' needs. He asks, "but whoever has the possession [things, material] of the world and sees his brother having need and closes his bowels of mercy from him, how does the love of God abide in him?" (3:17: *hos d' an echē ton bion tou kosmou*[160] *kai theōrē*[161] *ton adelphon autou chreian echonta kai kleisē ta splanchna*[162] *autou ap' autou, pōs hē agapē tou theou menei en autō*). The genitive *tou theou* (of God) qualifying *agapē* (love) here may be best taken as qualitative genitive in this context.[163] There

---

160. *Kosmos* (world) is here used to denote the place where we reside even as we wait to go to our eternal residence (heaven). When we are in the world, God blesses us differently. There are some who have more than they need while there are others who lack the basic things of life. John's point is that love is shown by sharing with, and not shutting out, those who lack those basics. Given the accumulation of wealth some have done, of the possessions of this world, it is quite possible that if all adhered to John's exhortation here, the poor would be reduced by a great fraction. Here is a challenge for those whom the Lord has blessed abundantly. He blesses us so that we can bless others.

161. The choice of words here is important. It is the one who has who sees the one who does not have, and then takes action to help. There have been many situations where someone who is not in need takes advantage of the kindness of someone else, amounting to "robbery" of some kind. This has in certain cases resulted in some not helping (as they should) those who come to their doors asking for assistance, in fear of being taken advantage of.

162. *Splanchna*, translated here as "bowels of mercy," represents that part of the body, within John's readers' worldview, that contains feelings for others. In our worldview, this can be equated with the heart. We usually say that our hearts were moved when we give reasons why we helped someone else.

163. Another possibility is objective genitive, that is, one who does not respond to a brother's or sister's need in a loving manner cannot claim to love God. This may find support, for example from 4:20. However, for the immediate context here where Jesus has been mentioned as the demonstration of what love is, the qualitative idea may be prominent.

Love as a Characteristic of a Believer (3:11–18)

is the love that is exemplified in the act of Christ and that is the love we are called to demonstrate as believers. This love makes the believer to respond with a helping hand when he or she is aware of a need a brother or sister has. None of us can give more than what Christ gave. He gave his own life, and we are here called to give only our possessions.

John, after repeating his address of his readers as *teknia* ("little children") concludes with the exhortation, "let us not love in word or with the tongue (only) but by deed and in truth" (3:18: *mē agapōmen*[164] *logō mēde tē glōssē alla en ergō kai aletheia*). The datives "word" (*logō*), "deed" (*ergō*), and "truth" (*aletheia*) focus on the manner of loving while "the tongue" (*tē glōssē*) focuses on the instrument of loving. The tongue can make any statements of love but unless that is accompanied by deeds, it does not amount to true love. It is very easy to tell someone, "I love you." It is another thing to show that by way of action. The talk of love must be confirmed by the walk of love.

The Wonderful Confidence (3:19–24)

> (3:19) And by this we will know that we are of the truth, and will convince[165] our heart[166] before him (have confidence in our heart before him) (20) whenever[167] the heart condemns us,[168] because

---

164. Here we have a hortatory subjunctive, expressing a general exhortation, with no judgment passed. It is to be the way of life for John, his readers, and everyone else who is willing to be exhorted.

165. In the context here, *peithō* seems to have the idea of overruling. The heart will be trying to pass wrong judgment but on the basis of God being greater, its judgment would be overruled. The act, however, is not one of harshness but of persuasion.

166. There is some awkwardness here as John combines the plural "our" with the singular "heart." What he may have in mind, though, could be that all of us who are believers will act accordingly, but each one dealing with his or her heart. In other words, the matter touches us all, but each is responsible individually. The use of "hearts" here (see for example, the Textus Receptus, represented in KJV) may therefore not be necessary in view of the lack of strong textual evidence to support it, among the manuscripts. For this and several other textual variations in this passage, see Painter 2003: 244–45.

167. There is some lack of clarity here because of two occurrences of *hoti* in 3:20, which if both are translated as "that" or "because" would not make sense. Some have preferred to leave out the first one but there is also the option of seeing a situation here where the first *hoti* is a misreading of *ho, ti*, followed by *ean* to give some translation of indefiniteness like "whatever" (that is, with respect to whatever the heart) or "whenever." For a more detailed discussion of this, see Baugh 1999: 60; and Culy 2004: 93–94.

168. The *hēmōn* of this phrase has been taken to be a genitive of direct object, rather

> God is greater than our heart and he knows all things. (21) Beloved, if our heart does not condemn us, we have boldness before God, (22) and whatever we ask we receive from him, because we keep his commandments and do the things that are pleasing in his sight. (23) And this is his commandment, that we believe in the name of his Son Jesus Christ and love one another, just as he gave a commandment to us. (24) And the one who keeps his commandments remains in him and he (remains) in him; and by this we know that he remains in us, out of the Spirit whom he gave to us.

There are two situations spelled out here: one in which our hearts[169] do not condemn us (in the sense that we are not conscious of anything wrong in our hearts that we have not put right—3:21) and another in which our hearts condemn[170] us, even after we have put things right with God (3:20). The first situation appeals to our clear conscience while the second situation appeals to the faithfulness of God, to forgive us once we have confessed our sins.

The pointer "by this" (*en toutō*) at the beginning of 3:19 points backward to 3:18 (loving by deed and in truth). When loving by deed and in truth is our habit, even in situations where our hearts may attempt to condemn us, we are free from condemnation and we can assert that "we are of the truth" (3:19a) and "have confidence" before God (3:19b). The basis for this confidence is not our emotional feeling (for at times we will feel like we are not forgiven or we have not done enough of helping) but the theological truths that "God is greater than our hearts" (3:20b: *meizōn estin ho theos tēs kardias hēmōn*). He is a more superior judge than our hearts and "he knows all things" (3:20c: *ginōskei*[171] *panta*). The "all" here is inclusive of our motives and intentions. Take, for example, a brother or sister who goes to speak to another brother/sister about an act of sin, with pure motive of correcting the sinning brother/sister, and then the brother/sister in sin attacks the concerned brother/sister as being judgemental. The attacked brother/

---

than possessive to read "our" as its other occurrences in 3:19-20.

169. Whether the use of heart here is to be taken as a synonym of conscience (Hobbs 1983: 93; Painter 2003: 248) or not (Kruse 2000: 139), it is clear that it has to do with "the inner life of the individual and his or her state of being" (Kysar 1986: 87). It is "the seat, not of emotions . . . but of the conscience and of self-knowledge" (Lieu 1991: 154).

170. Though this is a legal term, its focus here is "internal judgement rather than formal sentence" (Thomas 2004: 187). That is why God is brought in, not as a court of appeal but as the more superior judge.

171. We here have a customary present. It is God's unchangeable state to have full knowledge of all things. He is omniscient with regard to all things.

The Wonderful Confidence (3:19–24)

sister may go home feeling miserable and his/her heart almost accusing him/her for wrong doing. The remedy for such is to bring God in as judge. Since God is greater judge than our hearts and we believe he knows all things, and this includes that he knows our clean motive, then there should be no fear but assurance that God approves of us.[172] In truth, we walk and in true concern we sought to speak to the brother/sister who has chosen to take offence. This is different from our excusing ourselves even when we are in the wrong. Rather, it is calling God in when our hearts attempt to wrongly judge us.[173]

In relation to sharing our possessions with those who are in need (which John mentions here as a specific example), none of us can solve all the problems (needs) of the world, but collectively we can achieve much. John's point needs to be taken in terms of how each of us responds to the needs around our own contexts and in the measure God has blessed each one of us. If we allow our hearts to condemn us for needs we have no means to address, we would be unfair to ourselves. However, if we shut our feelings for one in need and we have the means to assist, John would judge us as having failed in the exercise of love.

The result of the second situation (that is, when our hearts do not condemn us) is that "we have boldness before God" (3:21: *parrēsian echomen*[174] *pros ton theon*) and "whatever we ask we receive from him" (3:22a:

---

172. Admittedly, this passage is certainly not totally clear in terms of its intention. Kruse, for example, limits its meaning to the act of helping our fellow believer in need. In other words, we know we should help but our hearts hold us back from doing so, and then "God being greater" is brought in as a warning that if we do not help in obedience to our mean hearts, God is greater than our heart and he will judge us (2000: 141). This understanding of *kataginōskein* (used twice in this passage, vv. 20 and 21) in the sense of hearts objecting to our rendering a helping hand is a bit difficult to comprehend. Its more natural meaning is "to condemn for a fault done." This is its meaning in Gal 2:11 also, the only other place it is used in the New Testament.

173. While this interpretation approaches the passage from the perspective that God overrules our hearts (conscience) to show more mercy, there are some (for example, Grayston 1984: 115) who take the view that God comes in as a stricter judge where our hearts are inclined to excuse us (see note 171 above also). Grayston sees the passage in light of the condemning tone set in 3:17–18. Also, see Kruse 2000: 141. In Kruse's understanding of the passage, 3:19–20 "functions as a stern warning against that meanness of heart which objects to our expending material resources to meet the needs of fellow believers, and provide a foil for the positive reinforcement of generosity offered in verses 21–22."

174. We here have a gnomic/customary present. It is the expected outcome of free conscience. It is a wonderful state to be when we approach God without any hesitation or shame.

ho ean aitōmen lambanomen[175] *ap' autou*). Here, we have our status (boldness before God) and our benefit/blessing (answer to our prayers). This happens when we do two things, namely, "we keep his commandments" (3:22b: *tas entolas autou tēroumen*[176]) and "do the things that are pleasing in his sight" (3:22c: *ta aresta enōpion autou poioumen*). These two conditions are the same thing said from different perspectives: one of them focusing on our obedience and the other on God's pleasure. God has given us his commandments, our response is supposed to be one of obedience, and our appropriate response receives God's positive response.

Two things summarize God's commandment—one of them touching belief (belief in the name of his Son Jesus Christ, *hina pisteusōmen*[177] *to onomati tou hyiou autou 'Iēsou Christou*[178]) and the other touching relationships, that is, "love for one another," *agapōmen*[179] *allēlous* (3:23). We cannot say that we believe in Jesus Christ and then proceed to not love one another, for it is the same Jesus who has given us the commandment to love. Love is at the center of his ideology.

The result of keeping this commandment is mystical union with Jesus. John expresses this in terms of remaining in Jesus and Jesus remaining in us (3:24). The actuality of this mystical union is not theoretical. It is real, for we have the Holy Spirit in our hearts.

When we have obeyed God, therefore, the expected outcome would be that our hearts would approve us. That may, however, not happen all the

175. Here is a futuristic present. The receiving is still future to the asking, but it is so certain that it is as well as done. This underlines the importance of a clear conscience as we deal with God, even in matters concerning our own needs.

176. Here is a durative present. It captures the "all the time" inclination of our hearts to obey God. It is not one time act of obedience, and it is also not annihilated by one act of sin followed by conviction and confession. It is what the heart is absorbed in. Hobbs puts it well when he says that Christians' "occasional sins of commission and omission are surface reactions; they do not reflect the deeper nature of the soul" (1983: 93).

177. The idea of believing in the name of someone has the notion of being emerged into that person's ideologies. In the New Testament sense, it has the idea of "placing faith in." Jesus is the object of faith, whom God has provided.

178. We here have an epexegetical genitive, stating more specifically who the Son to be believed in is. It is Jesus Christ and no other.

179. John's use of what tense, and where, is not without significance. When spelling out the specifics of the command, he uses the aorist tense for believing and the present tense for loving. The exercise of saving faith takes place at one given time in our lives (distinct from continued exercise of trust) but the act of loving becomes our way of life at all times. As Painter puts it, the aorist here signifies "the decisive nature of belief," while the present tense verb brings out "the continuous nature of the loving life" (2003: 245).

time. Our hearts could condemn us (by making us doubt whether what we have done has settled matters), instead of approving us. At those moments, our confidence in moving on in our Christian life is the assurance that God is greater than our hearts. He is the supreme judge on matters of our walk with him. As Schnackenburg says, "When Christians are condemned by their conscience, they not only recall that God knows their deeds of love; they hurl themselves into the ocean of the infinite understanding and mercy of God."[180] What a sure basis for confidence! There is no reason for us to allow Satan to use our confessed past to cripple us today. Once our merciful God clears our record by way of forgiveness, we are truly and forever clean concerning the forgiven sin.

The Clear Demarcation (4:1–6)

> (4:1) Beloved, do not believe every spirit, but test the spirits if they are of God, because many false prophets have gone out into the world. (2) By this we know the spirit of God; every spirit that confesses Jesus Christ as having come[181] in flesh is of God, (3) and every spirit that does not confess Jesus is not of God; and this is the (spirit) of the antichrist, which you have heard that it comes, and now is in the world already (4) You yourselves[182] are of God,

---

180. Schnackenburg 1992: 186.

181. Most translations (NASB, NIV, KJB, HCSB and others) translate the perfect participle (*elēlythota*) here as "has come," that is, taking its function as an independent participle. The choice of "as having come" (taking the function of the participle as supplementary, complementing the verb "confess") has been made here so as to capture John's intention in this verse as more the manner in which he came (he came in flesh) than the event (that is, what did he do?). This understanding of John here is also what Brooke has in mind when he says, "The phrase describes the method rather than the fact. The revelation of God was made to men by the Son of God appearing in human form and living a human life" (1912: 109). This is also supported by the fact that John had the choice to use the perfect indicative (*elēluthe*) as he does elsewhere in the epistle (for example, *metabebēkamen* in 3:14 and *nenikēkate* in 4:4, among others) but he used a participle. If "has come" is the right rendering here, it would be the only place in 1 John where we have independent use (a participle functioning as an indicative or imperative) of a participle.

182. It could be debated whether a nominative pronoun (for example *hēmeis* and *humeis*) used with a verb to be (in this case, *este*) is emphatic or not (for example, Baugh 1999: 64, says it is not) but the context must play a key role in determining this. In this context, John has a dualism that runs throughout the passage. There is God and the world, we and the false teachers, you and them, truth and falsehood, just to mention some of the primary ones. Emphasis of "we" (4:6), "you" (4:4), and "they" (4:5) would not be out of order (See also Thomas 2004: 206–7).

children, and you have overcome them, because greater is the one in you than the one in the world. (5) They are of the world; because of this they speak of the world and the world hears them (6) We ourselves are of God; the one who knows God hears us, who is not of God does not hear us. Out of this we know the spirit of truth and the spirit of lie.

We have in this passage both a prohibition ("do not believe," *mē pisteuete*) and a command ("test," *dokimazete*).[183] The object of the prohibition (expressed using *mē* and present imperative[184]) is *panti pneumati*[185] ("every spirit," that is, every spirit as they come our way) and the object of the command is *ta pneumata* ("the spirits," that is, all of them). The alarm is caused by the fact that "many false prophets[186] have gone[187] into

---

183. One may wonder whether John is here commanding or entreating his readers (functions that are both served by the imperative mood) given the endearing address (*agapētoi*, beloved) he uses for them. If we adopt the position taken on the accompanying prohibition that some of the believers were becoming gullible to the false teachings, seeing it as command is a very reasonable position. His commanding tone would not dilute his love for them.

184. The use of *mē* and present imperative in contexts of prohibition is usually to stop an action still in progress. However, also see discussion under notes 102 and 151. Nonetheless, to render it as "do not keep believing," as Thomas (2004: 198) suggests, begs the question whether they should believe every spirit occasionally. Working with the traditional position on this matter, this would mean that John's readers were opening the doors of their belief without the needed discrimination to determine the bearers of doctrinal truth and the bearers of falsehood. They should stop doing so.

185. The case here is dative because *pisteuō* is one of those Greek verbs that take dative for direct object.

186. The duties of a prophet in the biblical sense is to forth tell (what is already revealed) more than to foretell (what is not revealed to others). This may be the reverse of the common use today where when one says he/she is a prophet, there is expectation for him/her to tell us about tomorrow. Within the Johannine scenario, it means that there were many out there proclaiming falsehood as opposed to truth.

187. The perfect tense used here (*exelēlythasin*) has as its focus, in this context, the existing results of what has taken place (intensive shade of the perfect). The false prophets are out there, desiring to spread their falsehood. Also to be noted is that, though the "going out" here can be understood in light of 2:19 (*ex hēmōn exēlthan*, out of us they went) it does not need to be limited to that. They could have gone out from Johannine and other communities of believers (viewing it from the perspective of the total context of the sphere in which God reigns) into the world. John is not just concerned about some Johannine traditions but the truth as it was passed on by the witness bearers he introduced in 1:1–4.

The Clear Demarcation (4:1–6)

the world"[188] (4:1b) and if one believes all of the spirits,[189] some will be[190] in error. At the same time, if one throws all of them away, the one to bring blessings may be cast out too.[191] This is a caution against wholesale acceptance or wholesale condemnation, even if at the outset we sense agreement or disagreement with our position. Our "testing instruments" must always be on the alert.[192] We can liken this in our everyday life, for example, to buying a light bulb. We (at least most of us) do not just take to the counter and pay for the first one our hand lays hold of in a supermarket. We place it where we expect it to light. If it lights, we buy it. If it does not light, it is no good for us or for anyone else. Until we test it though, we should not throw it away.[193]

The standard John spells out here is whether the spirit is of God[194] or it is not. This is because there are other spirits out there, including that

---

188. World, in this context, represents the sphere that operates under Satan, in opposition to the sphere in which God reigns.

189. John connects "spirits" here with "false prophets" in a manner that implies he is not thinking of spirits in the sense of demons. It makes better sense if they are perceived as human "impulses that are not of God" (Jobes 2014: 177). In other words, what John has in mind here are "individuals who function in a prophetic capacity" (Thomas 2004: 200) and are not led by the Spirit of God but by the spirit of the antichrist.

190. The predictive future is used here because if there are false prophets out there, then presence of falsehood is guaranteed.

191. This is much so, because John's teaching on spirits to be discerned here may be building (in his thoughts) on the mention of the Spirit in 3:24, where he has talked of the Spirit as imparting knowledge to those who remain faithful to the truth.

192. Though the testing will be applied as the spirits arise (taking *dokimazete* as iterative present), the instrument for testing them will be on all the time (durative idea). False teachings do not give us warnings before they come. This is why we should all be like the believers of Berea (Acts 17:11), taking everything we read, hear, and see through the test of sound doctrine.

193. Use of light bulb here is just one example. The same is applied when we are buying a biro (does it write?), mobile phone (does it have functioning features?), and many other things. Testing is the common sense thing to do in everyday life. One, however, has also to do it with care. One day I went to buy a washing basin with a young man (with strong hands) and in testing the first one (by squeezing it to see how strong it is), he broke it (we assumed it had been in the sun for too long). The seller insisted that we had to pay for it. Falsehood, therefore, can also go with trickery. Some people can say what appears to be false, not because they believe it but because they want to watch our reactions. They enjoy seeing us react out of proportion. We need wisdom to discern their motive.

194. While this is the idea here (that is, "is it the spirit of God or is it of the antichrist?") the literal idea of the Greek (*ei ek tou theou estin*) can be expressed more strongly to keep the idea of source. In other words, has the spirit been sent by God or not? The only way such a test can be done is by comparing its proclamation with what God has said in the

of the antichrist.[195] While John here uses "antichrist" in the singular, this does not mean his concern is that of the "antichrist" yet to come within our study of eschatology.[196] Any spirit that is against Christ has as its "father" or "mother" the single antichrist yet to come. Within the context here, the false prophets represent the spirit of the antichrist.[197] By implication also, even the teachings within our own times that do not promote, but rather fight Christ, are included. The prohibition and exhortation here, therefore, apply to them as well.

The test given here[198] is what is said about Jesus Christ having come in the flesh (4:2). John uses confession of Jesus (4:3) as a parallel thought to confession of Jesus Christ having come in the flesh (4:2). One can view the expression in 4:3 (confessing Jesus) as the one to control the first one (confess that Jesus Christ came in the flesh) and so understand what John has in mind here as Jesus' saving mission.[199] In other words a denial of what John is guarding here would be a denial of Jesus' salvific ministry in his "incarnate life, death, and resurrection on behalf of the human race."[200] Another option, however, and this is preferred by the present writer, is to understand the confession of Jesus in 4:3 in light of the confession that

---

Scriptures, his word. If anything contradicts what the Scripture teaches, then it cannot be sent by God for he cannot contradict himself.

195. The term *antichristos* (antichrist) is a Johannine term, found in 1 John 2:18, 22; 4:3; and 2 John 7 (also see notes 115 and 120). The view taken in this work is that the force of the preposition "*anti*" in the title is more "against" than "instead of." The false teachers in John are presented as attacking the truth concerning Christ.

196. The man of lawlessness Paul talks of in 2 Thess 2:3 is still a future figure. If this figure and John's figure of antichrist are the same person (see note 119), then there is still a full realization of this event that is beyond the time of the false teachers John was confronting here.

197. While the description "of God" (describing spirit) here is best taken as genitive of source (sent by God/from God), the description "of the antichrist" could be qualitative genitive (spirit as of the antichrist).

198. For John's original readers, the specific matter was the nature of Christ. The principle he lays here, however, can be applied to other deviations from the truth of Scripture as they come in different times in history. When tested and found not to pass the test of sound doctrine, they must be rejected.

199. This understanding of John here builds on the answer for the question "what do I do to be saved?" with the answer being "believe in the Lord Jesus" (Acts 16:30–31). While this was the answer given by Paul and Silas, it was a standard reply to this question for it is based on Jesus' own claim to be the "way, the truth and the life" (John 14:6).

200. Jobes 2014: 178. Also Schnackenburg 1992: 201; and Thomas 2004: 203; among others.

The Clear Demarcation (4:1–6)

Jesus Christ came in the flesh in 4:2. This shifts the focus from Jesus' mission of saving to Jesus' nature. Who is he? Jesus Christ combines his ordinariness (Jesus) and his extraordinariness (Christ). The one person who is both human and divine came in the flesh. Failure to confess Jesus (4:3), therefore, amounts to a denial of his humanity,[201] which in 4:2 is expressed as "coming in the flesh." What this amounts to can be viewed within the context of Gnosticism though only in terms of its un-unified elements (see comment under 2:22 also). Docetism and Ebionism expressions of the error in particular were present during the time John wrote the epistle. For John and other true prophets, however, the two natures (divine and human) are united in the one person. It is only in his capacity as God that he would achieve what is needed in redemption, and it is only in his capacity as man that he qualifies to be a suitable savior for humankind. The two natures of Christ (divine and human) are not only Scripturally true, but also logically necessary.

The matter of who Jesus is divides prophets into two categories, in this context. There are those who have the spirit of truth, which comes from God and asserts that Jesus Christ came in flesh (Jesus is the Christ or Christ is Jesus, depending on the kind of error under correction, the point is made from[202]) while there are those with the spirit of lies that comes from the world (the sphere Satan rules) that denies this fact about Jesus. John belongs to those with spirit of truth[203] while the false prophets have "the spirit of lies" (*to pneuma tēs planēs*[204]).

In our theological discussions today, we meet the question of whether "Jesus of history" is the same as "Christ of faith" (see n. 201 also). This issue

---

201. Some of those who see the focus of John's point here as a denial of Jesus' humanity include Kruse (2000: 147) and Yarbrough (2008: 223).

202. The Jews struggled with the identification of Jesus as the Christ (the Messiah) while the Greeks struggled with tracing the Christ in all its fullness (the object of worship) to Jesus. It is the latter that is at the center of current struggle in New Testament scholarship today. Christ of faith is not denied but cannot be identified as the same person as the historical Jesus. There is some relationship but not equation. The belief attached to Christ is artificial product from what some chose to believe about Jesus. Such views about Jesus would be termed by John as *ek tou kosmou* (of the world) and not *ek tou theou* (originating with God) as he has revealed himself in the Scriptures.

203. In 4:6a, John makes an emphatic claim, *hēmeis ek tou theou esmen* (we [ourselves] are of God). They represent his true emissaries. The "we" includes the other apostles (see discussion on use of first person plural in 1:1–4) and those who are faithful to their teachings like his readers.

204. This is an objective genitive. The spirits produce lies. That is what they teach.

may not have been articulated the way it is in our times, but the effect of the issue was the same. Who is the Jesus we worship? Is he God become man or is it a man raised in our praises to the level of being worshipped? John says that a denial of his human nature is not from the spirit of God. By the same token, a spirit that denies his divine nature is not of God. Jesus' two natures is a scriptural truth we must not only believe but also defend.

Those who are God's children will listen to John (whose teaching is that God became flesh and dwelt among us—John 1:14) and those who teach what he proclaims, while those who are of the world will not hear John and his followers (4:5). In fact, those who are of the world will be hostile to John and his followers. There is no need for fear, however, because "greater is the one" in the faithful than the one in the world (4:4). The greater one here could be the Holy Spirit[205] or Jesus[206] (or even God the Father[207] in view of similar phrasing in 3:20) but Jesus is a better choice since he is the one John talks of as having overcome the world (John 16:33) and in this passage (4:4) he talks of the faithful as having overcome those who are hostile to the truth.

This situation can be multiplied in different contexts. The tension between truth and falsehood does not belong to one generation but is there all the time. The issues at times may not be theological but ethical, but they will always be there. The point is, if we stand with God there is no cause for alarm. When God is on our side, who can overcome us? No one! God may allow falsehood to have the appearance of success, but that is only for a time and for his mysterious purposes. Truth always has the final say for God is in the camp of truth.

THE TRIANGLE OF LOVE (4:7–21)[208]

> (4:7) Beloved, let us love one another, because love is of God, and everyone who loves has been born of God and knows (*ginōskei*)

---

205. Burge 1996: 176; Kruse 2000: 148; Bruce 1970: 106; Stott 1964: 157; and Burdick 1985: 307.
206. Yarbrough 2008: 227; and Kistemaker 1986: 328.
207. Kysar 1986: 92; Painter 2003: 261; and Brooke 1912: 114.
208. The three corners of the triangle are God, man/woman, and neighbor. Each connecting line has two way traffic, God loving both man/woman and man/woman's neighbor while each of them loves God in response, and they also love each other.

The Triangle of Love (4:7–21)

God. (8) The one who does not love has not known[209] God, because God is love. (9) In this the love of God was manifested for us,[210] that God sent[211] his only begotten Son into the world in order that we might be saved through him. (10) In this is love, not that we (ourselves) loved[212] God but that he (himself) loved us and sent his Son (as[213]) propitiation for our sins. (11) Beloved, since[214] in this manner God loved us, we (ourselves) also ought to love one another. (12) No one has seen God at any time. If we love one another, God remains in us and his love has been perfected[215] in us. (13) By this we know that we remain in him and he in us, because of his Spirit he has given to us. (14) and we (ourselves) have seen (him) and we bear witness that the Father has sent the Son (as) Savior[216] of the world. (15) Whoever confesses that Jesus is the Son of God, God remains in him and he (remains) in God. (16) And we (ourselves) have known (*egnōkamen*) and have believed[217] the love which God has for us.[218]

God is love, and the one who remains in love remains in God and God remains in him. (17) In this, love has been perfected with[219] us, in order that we may have boldness on the day of judg-

---

209. This (*has not known*) translates an aorist tense (*egnō*) but is given a perfect equivalent translation (*has not known*) because it is determined to be resultative aorist. The translation "does not know" is also possible if the aorist *egnō* is taken to be gnomic.

210. The use of *en hēmin* here and also in 4:16 is best, from context, translated "for us" with the basic idea being "with reference to us" (that is, dative of respect or reference). Both "in/within us" and "among us" would make little sense.

211. This (*sent*) translates a perfect tense here. While "has sent" is also a possible translation, "sent" makes better sense, taking the perfect tense as intensive in shade.

212. The Greek verb here (*loved*) is also a perfect tense, in the Greek text. Instead of translating it as "have loved," "loved" has been used as it makes better sense, taking it as intensive in shade.

213. Taking *hilasmon* (propitiation) as accusative of "reference."

214. We have a first class condition here. It is true God loved us in the special manner specified in the context.

215. John uses a periphrastic construction here, to emphasize this reality.

216. Another accusative of "reference," as *hilasmon* in v. 10.

217. The two perfect verbs, *egnōkamen* and *pepisteukamen*, focus on our status (result).

218. Another remote meaning of *en*, meaning "for." See v. 9 also.

219. While some translations prefer to take the preposition *meta* that we have here, in the Greek, as having a remote meaning (for example the NIV translates it as "among") the usual translation of it as "with" still makes sense. God loved us and sent his Son to die for us, loves us as his children, and his abiding in us completes that process. The focus, however, is not on "how much" since God loves perfectly all the time, but what he does.

ment, because just as he is,[220] we (ourselves) also are in this world. (18) There is no fear in love but perfect love casts out fear, because fear has (an element of) punishment, and the one who fears has not been perfected in love. (19) We (ourselves) love, because he (himself) first loved us. (20) If anyone says, "I love God" and hates his brother, he is a liar; for the one who does not love his brother whom he has seen, is not able to love God whom he has not seen. (21) And we have this commandment from him, that the one who loves God also ought to love[221] his brother.

This is the third major passage on love in this epistle. The earlier ones include 2:7–17 (entitled in this work as "The Ageless Commandment—Old Yet New") and 3:11–18 (entitled in this work as "Love, a Distinctive Characteristic of a Believer"). While this passage is definitely a repetition of the same theme, I agree with Thomas who says, it is not "a mere repetition."[222] Apart from repetition for emphasis, there is also a development of thought. The first two passages approach love with emphasis on an ethical perspective. It is the duty of the believer. In this third passage, John seeks to "fortify the theological foundation of the imperative to love."[223] As will be discussed below, love is not only defined by God but also demonstrated by him, before it is demanded from the believer.

In the passage we find love expressed in three dimensions: God's love for us, our love for God, and our love for one another. We can refer to this as vertical love, response love, and horizontal love, respectively. The three also constitute a mystical union that is a mystery of God's own working.

Vertical Love

John here lays emphasis on believers as the object of God's love though we know that God exercises his love to all of humankind.[224] In his relationship

The focus here is on his remaining in us. There is a lasting fellowship with him.

220. The idea is that as God is love and we are in him and he in us, we are love to the world, as extension of him.

221. The literal translation of the Greek here is "also loves" but from the context, given that it is a command, "ought to love" makes better sense, taking the verb *agapa* as a cohortative indicative.

222. Thomas 2004: 214.

223. Yarbrough 2008: 235.

224. Such passages as John 3:16 and Gal 2:20c place the act of love before redemption but there is always a special relationship God has with those who have been born of him

with us "love" defines[225] who he is and dictates[226] what he does. He is also its source.[227]

When John says that "God is love" (4:8, 16) he does not mean to equate God with love for we know that he is also holy[228] (the basis of his justice, including judgement) but to assert that all his deeds (whether blessing or punishing) spring from love. There is nothing he does that lacks love dimension.[229] It could sound like a mystery, for God is also said to hate sin (Isa 61:8; Rev 2:6) but even that very act is done out of love. In biblical terms, love is not a pat on the back, but even when it is a spank, it is done for the good of the recipient. We cannot, therefore, say that God is love (blessing) on one hand and holy (judging) on the other, but rather he is "Holy-Love" at the same time. In all his acts, the two elements of his nature go together. It is only that the focus here is on the element of love.

God's act of sending his Son served both a legal purpose and as a demonstration of love. In 4:9, John says that God sent the Son "so that we might be saved through him" (*hina zēsōmen di' autou*) and in 4:10, he says that the Son was sent as "a propitiation for our sins" (*hilasmon peri tōn amartiōn hēmōn*). Though the word translated propitiation here, *hilasmos*, is debated how it should be best understood (see discussion under 2:2), the element of responding to God's wrath by means of meeting the demands of justice cannot be left out of it. God's Son died on the cross so that by his death the demands of God's holiness against our sins would be satisfied. He appeased God, taking away God's anger toward us and providing a way by means of

---

through faith in Christ.

225. Twice (4:8, 16) in this passage John says, *ho theos agapē estin* (God is love).

226. John uses the fact that God sent his only Son into the world to pay penalty for our sins as a demonstration of his love (4:9, 10, 14).

227. In 4:7, John uses the expression, *he agapē ek tou theou estin* (literally, "love is out of God"). It springs out of his very nature. Our union with him makes it possible for us to love as we should.

228. While the exact words are used by Peter (1 Pet 1:15), it is the same idea John expressed when he says that God is light in 1:5.

229. The assertion is deeper than stating an attribute of God, as loving, and not as deep as a statement of his identity. It fits more within the level of a nickname. For example, my mother whose official name was Tabitha Kanukwa was also called Mutheu as a nickname. Mutheu (literally means "clean") was given to her because of her determination to keep everything around her in a state of cleanliness. In a similar way, when John says "God is love" he is not asking us to exchange "God" with "love" but to perceive all his deeds as controlled by this virtue. Brooke puts it well, "Love is not merely an attribute of God, it is His very Nature and Being" (1912: 118).

which we become God's beloved. By God's Son's act, we (believers) were saved from God's wrath, now and forever.

In 4:11, John makes an appeal for believers to love each other on the basis of God's act of sending his Son. Using a first class condition, he says, "if (since) God loved[230] us in this manner, we also ought to love[231] one another." John emphasizes the high degree of God's love by stating whom he sent. It was his own son, and the only Son for that matter (4:9). He could spare nothing at all, not even his beloved Son. There is no greater love than this. In response for what God did, we love him and also love his people.

While God's love for us is perfect, it is not static. John brings out the matter of God remaining in us, as we are in him, as a perfecting of this love he has for us (4:17). Using human relationships, the statement of "I do" on the day of a wedding is not the ultimate expression of love, though perfect in itself. There is the living together that follows, and where there is harmony, each act of love in the relationship contributes to making the love even deeper. Love is more an act of sharing of self than a feeling.

Response Love

By this, we mean our love for God on the basis of his love for us. Though this is not as emphasized in this passage as vertical love (see above) and horizontal love (see below), there are certain statements that John makes that need to be noted. In 4:19, John says, "we love because he first loved us" (*hēmeis agapōmen*,[232] *hoti autos prōtos ēgapēsen hēmas*). Our love for God or for the rest of his creation is in response to what he did. Unless we have him setting the example, we would totally be lost in the exercise of this virtue. What we know is to love our own selves selfishly and that is all

---

230. The translation "loved" for *ēgapēsen* is called for by the context, since it relates to the historical event of God sending his Son. However, "loves" is also a possible translation if one takes the aorist *ēgapēsen* to be gnomic. God loves as that is his nature and loved us in the practical manner of sending his Son to take away our sins.

231. The present tense (*agapan*) is used here. Loving is to be our way of life as God's recipients of his love.

232. The verb *agapōmen* does not have a direct object, either God or his creation. This could be deliberate so that it covers love in a comprehensive sense. Love (*agapē* love) is a discipline and we, as fallen men and women, would not be able to exercise it if we never got the lesson on what it is all about from God himself. At the same time, we also have the obligation to exercise it because we are beneficiaries of it. Receiving creates an obligation to give the same. The emphatic *hēmeis* (we ourselves) and *autos* (he himself) are also to be noted. God is the teacher and we are the students, to learn about love.

we can do without learning from the example God has set for us to follow. In 4:20, John also mentions a possible claim to love God, though he says it must go with the horizontal love. Not to love God in response to his act of love toward us would be the highest degree of ingratitude, yet more attention is given to our extending our love to fellow human beings. This is the horizontal relationship to which we now turn.

Horizontal Love

Strange enough, John does not say "since in this manner God loved us" we ought "to love him back" but rather he says, "we ought to love one another" (4:11). This could be, because God does not need our love to live full life (he remains God with all his attributes no matter what anyone does or says; he needs no one to defend him) but we and our fellow human beings do. Our emotions and well-being are tied to other people's acceptance of us. We need each other to live full lives.

The need for this horizontal love is placed at the very beginning of this passage, "Beloved, let us love one another" (4:7a). We have a hortatory subjunctive (*agapōmen*, let us love) whose goal is to call the believers (*agapētoi*,[233] "beloved") into loving attitudes and actions toward one another. John gives the basis of this call as that "love is of God, and everyone who loves has been born of God and knows God" (4:7a). In other words, this is the expectation in the family of God.[234] It is not uncommon for families

---

233. This (*agapētos/agapētoi*) is John's favorite title in this epistle (3:2, 21; 4:1, 7, 11) for those who are living out the truth they have received from him and other apostles. It is also found in 3 John 1, 2, 5, and 11, making it a total of nine times in the two epistles, out of a total of sixty-two times in the New Testament.

234. We are God's extension (born of God) and that is why, for John, to be born of God and not love is a "no, no." We are extension of God wherever love of this kind is found. This is not to equate God, in his essence, with love in any abstract sense but rather to say that God is a God in revelation and revelation is action. Brooke puts it well, "The proper result of divine birth is divine activity" (1912: 120). For John in this passage, that activity is the exercise of love. He is not only love, but also "light" (1 John 1:5: *ho theos phōs estin*) and "spirit" (John 4:24: *pneuma ho theos*) in the writings of John. We here have the "trinity of God's nature." He is love, he is light, and he is spirit. In his revelation he is also "Father," "Son," and "Holy Spirit." In a sense then, love focus equals the Father focus; light focus equals the Son focus (he brings out what God is), and spirit focus equals Holy Spirit focus (he works in the lives of believers). This is why John says we know God as love by the Spirit he has given us (4:13). Focus (above) is emphasized because what one of the Persons of the Trinity is does not exclude the other Persons. There is a mysterious oneness yet each has his focus in effecting and applying redemption.

to have certain characteristics that are known to be part of their members. Without any attempt to stereotype, there are certain life characteristics that seem to go with different nationalities and within those nationalities, families have certain traits also. Love is an expected life quality of everyone who has been born of God and claims to know God. The continual practice of loving sacrificially affirms that one has been born of God and knows God.[235] The focus of the perfect *gegennētai* ("has been born") is the result,[236] the status of being a child of God. The act of knowing (*ginōskei*, "he knows") here is not just the matter of having some ideas about, but having deep relationship with—to the point of knowing the likes and dislikes of the person. Love for one another, therefore, becomes a testimony of our status and relationship with God. When the people of God throw love out of the window, it not only makes a statement about them but also about their knowledge of the God they claim to serve. The church is better off with two ministers of the word who live in accordance with the constitution of the kingdom of God than with hundred ministers who do not love each other. In fact John says, "the one who does not love does not know God" (4:8). He further says, "the one who does not love his brother whom he has seen, is not able to love God whom he has not seen" (4:20). There is, therefore, no need of having ministers of the word of God who do not know or love God. To know God is to know that he is love and to love God is to obey him, and his will is for us to love one another. The place of love among us as believers cannot be overemphasized. God is love and those who serve him must love each other.

This horizontal relationship is also placed at the close of this passage (4:21). In other words, the whole passage is sandwiched between the exhortation to love ("let us love one another," 4:7) and a reminder that this is a commandment: "and we have this commandment from him, that the one who loves God loves (ought to love) his brother also" (4:21). John is most likely here alluding to the golden twin rule from Jesus himself: "You shall love the Lord your God with all your heart . . . and you shall love your neighbor as yourself" (Matt 22:37; Mark 12:30; Luke 10:27). Love whose object is *theos* (God) goes together with love for *plēsion* (neighbor).[237] Love

---

235. In 4:7 we have the present subjunctive *agapōmen* (let us love) and the present participle *agapōn* (loves). The present participle is used again in 4:8, 20 and 21. The act of loving expected of us toward each other is expressed using a present tense throughout the passage.

236. In other words, we here have intensive perfect.

237. The word for neighbor comes from the adverb "near" (*plēsion*). The context

for neighbor without love for God cannot be *agapē* type of love (a love that sacrifices no matter the circumstances, not a love that works on basis of conditions to be met) and love for God without love for neighbor is not complete love, or as Jobes says, it has not been "brought to its intended goal and fullest form."[238] This is why in Jesus' teaching he also instructs that when we go before God to worship him and as we do so remember that there is a matter at the horizontal level that is not right with our neighbor, we first go and take care of it and then come to finish our worship (Matt 5:23–24). Worship within the context of hurting relationships cannot be worship, for the twin commandment of love is not a reality. May the Lord help his church to make right the many broken relationships, so that its worship will be acceptable before the Lord!

Mystery of This Love

Within the sandwich, there is in 4:12–19 what appears to be a digression but is in actuality a deep reflection on what this kind of love (*agapē*) means for the Persons of the Trinity and the believer.

The point of the passage may be illumined by our thinking of a marriage relationship.[239] There are the marriage parties, who are God and the believer.[240] There is the one who pays the bride (purchasing) price, namely,

---

defines this nearness. Within the context of spiritual nearness, the terms "brother" or "sister" (*adelphos, adelphē*) are appropriate. There is some spiritual kinship. The principles governing relationship with one of them ("neighbor" and "brother" or "sister"), however, apply to the other also. When the Scripture has special reason to ask that a particular thing apply more within the spiritual kinship, it uses "especially those who are believers" (Gal 6:10; 1 Tim 4:10), which by implication means that the "neighbor" in the general sense is not excluded from being a recipient of love.

238. Jobes 2014: 195.

239. John does not mention marriage here but the institution of marriage provides a physical union that can also illumine some dynamics of a spiritual union. Also, John talks of believers as begotten and not as betrothed to God (though betrothed to Christ, Rev 21:9). The relationship that is established, however, has a present reality and future expectation that is best shown within the context of marriage institution. The idea of God and the believer being in union is found in 4:12 (*ho theos en hēmin menei*, "God remains in us"), 13 (*en autō menomen kai autos en hēmin*, "we remain in him and he in us"), 15 (*ho theos en autō menei kai autos en tō theō*, "God remains in him and he in God"), and 16 (*en tō theō menei kai ho theos en autō menei*, "he remains in God and God remains in him"). In 4:17, he talks of confidence of the believer on the day of judgement.

240. In 4:15, John talks of God remaining (*menei*) in the believer and the believer remaining in God. The same thought is repeated in 4:16. This communicates of a deep

the Son, sent by the Father. In 4:14, using a "we" that includes all believers, John says that we have seen and we testify that God sent his Son as Savior of the world. We, therefore, have no doubt that the bride price to make us God's own has been paid. There is also the engagement ring,[241] assuring us that we belong to God. In 4:13, the Spirit whom God has given to us serves as the basis for our knowledge (*en toutō ginōskomen*) that we remain (*menomen*) in him and he remains in us.[242] In other words, the marriage plans are firm. There is the anticipated future union against which the believer has confidence, not fear. This is because we have known (*egnōkamen*) and we have believed (*pepisteukamen*) the love which God has with (*en*) us (4:16). God is not playing a game with us. He is seriously our marriage partner.[243] The only conditions we need to meet are to remain in love (4:16b: *ho menōn en tē agapē*, "the one who remains in love") and confess that Jesus is the Son of God (4:15: *hos ean homologēsē hoti Iesous estin ho hyios tou theou*, "the one who confesses that Jesus is the Son of God"). A second reason why there is no fear is that love excludes fear (4:18a). Fear is cast out by perfect love (4:18b).

While in this world (that is, the time we now live) God is in love with us, and we (the believers) are in love with God (*kathōs ekeinos estin kai hēmeis esmen*, "just as he is, also we are," 4:17b). In this union with him the love he has with us (*meth' hēmon*) is perfected to the extent that on the day of judgment, we will have confidence (4:17a). The day of judgment will usher in, for us believers, perfection of love, and by extension absence of fear (4:18). In our days on earth, we therefore do not obey God because of fear but because we are lovers with him. On the day of judgment, we will not face him with fear, but with confidence.

John reminds his readers that this spiritual union is not man introduced but God initiated.[244] In 4:19, he says, "we love, because he first loved

---

fellowship God has with those who have been begotten by him.

241. While not all cultures of the world use rings for engagement most do, and where there is no engagement, there is an equivalent act that affirms to all concerned the seriousness of the bridegroom about the relationship.

242. Brooke says, "By means of the Spirit . . . we are conscious that fellowship between Him and us really exists" (1912: 120–21).

243. God being our marriage partner is not in contradiction with the Son being our marriage partner. In the mystery of the Trinity, the Father and the Son are one. What is said, and where, depends on what the emphasis of a passage (or author) is. Paul, in Eph 5:32, talks of Christ as the bridegroom but here John emphasizes our union with God.

244. Traditionally, for both Jews and some other cultures, especially in Africa, a

The Triangle of Love (4:7–21)

us." This is why in 4:7 John had said that the love he is talking about here is from God. God gives it to us, and then we respond—whether loving him or loving our fellow human beings.

This mystical spiritual union has some ministerial function. At level one, God loves and shows it by sending his Son (4:10, 14). At level two, we extend this kind of love to God in gratitude (4:19) and to fellow members of humankind in obedience to God's commandment to love. As we love one another, we proclaim God (who is invisible, 4:12) who is love. Our act of loving completes the process of expressing love. God started it by sending his Son, and the believers complete it by loving each other (4:12b).

That is to say, God who is love is lived out by us when we love one another, and as we do so we are completing (perfecting) the revelation of what he is, namely, love.[245]

Summary

This is, admittedly, a difficult passage in terms of how all ideas connect to love. Kruse (commenting on 4:7—5:4 as a unit) says, "The structure of this passage and the progression of thought within it are difficult to explain, even though the smaller units which make it up are easy to identify."[246] Its message (in this work limiting it to 4:21), however, can be summarized as follows.

The very being of God can be expressed by the term "love" (*agapē*). Love is not only his nature but also permeates his dealings with human beings. Its highest degree of expression is seen in his sending his only Son to be Savior—by meeting the demands of justice and paying with his own life. Those who have been born of God share his nature and so are called to love. The act of loving serves as a confirmation that we have been born of

---

marriage relationship began with the man (or his representative) not the woman proposing and the woman responding to the proposal. This initial move, however, gives birth to a mutual exchange of love. Within the marriage relationship itself, each party gives itself to the other in love. In the same way, God extends his love to us, and John exhorts that we should respond to this act of God with both gratitude and full surrender to him, in love.

245. This can be put in a graphic way (within context of general theology) as follows: God reveals himself in nature (general revelation), in the Scriptures (special revelation), in Christ (the ultimate act of love), and in the community of believers ("loving in response and horizontally"—love for God and love for others go together). That is, when we love, as God does, we reveal God. Since God is love, his revelation which began with creation is perfected (brought to its end point, in application) in our acts of love.

246. Kruse 2000: 156.

God and know him. Those who do not love do not know God, and if they make the claim to do so, they are lying.

While God is eternally and by nature "love" we are his instruments, on this world, to carry on further that love. As we love one another, we are completing the God-started process of loving. The act of loving also unites us with God in such a manner that we have confidence when we approach him, even in time of judgment. God has given us his Spirit as assurance that as long as we confess Jesus is the Son of God, and exercise love to others, we have a lasting fellowship with him. This is a union (marriage) that is God-initiated, God-executed, and God-guarded. Ours is to respond in faith and in obedience, based on love and not fear.

THE FINAL TEST (5:1–5)[247]

> (5:1) Everyone who believes that Jesus is the Christ has been born of God, and everyone who loves the one that has begotten loves (also) the one who has been begotten by (out of) him. (2) By this we know that we love the children of God, whenever we love God and do his commandments. (3) For this is the love of God, that we keep his commandments; and his commandments are not burdensome, (4) because everyone who has been born of God overcomes the world; and this is the victory which overcomes[248] the world, our faith (5) and who is it who overcomes the world, except the one who believes that Jesus is the Son of God?

In the same manner that the preceding portion (4:7–21) was sandwiched between the matter of love (4:7: "Let us love one another"; 4:21: "And we have this commandment from him, that the one who loves God also loves his brother") this passage is sandwiched between two statements of belief. In 5:1 we have the belief that "Jesus is the Christ" (*Iēsous estin ho Christos*) and in 5:5 "Jesus is the Son of God" (*Iēous estin ho hyios tou*

---

[247]. The word "final" here is used with double meaning. When within the structure of 1 John one talks of tests, there are the moral test (righteousness with focus on love) and theological test (see for example, Keener 1993: 737 and 739; and Carson and Moo 2005: 670). This is the last passage in which John provides a test as to who has been born of God. At a second level, "final" is here used in the sense of "comprehensive examination" in which all that has been learned is tested. In this passage, John puts together both the moral and theological tests.

[248]. This (overcomes) translates an aorist, determined here to be a gnomic aorist. It's the nature of faith to overcome.

The Final Test (5:1–5)

theou). Belief that Jesus is the Christ is related to the one that "has been born of God" (*ek theou gegennētai*) while the belief that Jesus is the Son of God is related to the one "who overcomes the world" (*ho nikōn ton kosmon*). For both statements of belief the present tense is used (*ho pisteuōn*). These two statements of belief are important for John, as we find the second (Jesus is the Son of God) also in 4:15 (cf. 4:2, 3) and both statements in his Gospel (John 20:31). While it is doubtful John wants to make too much difference between the two pairs, there could be a reason why new birth is related to *Chistos* while victory is related to *hyios tou theou* (Son of God) here. Being the Christ means there is no other like him, for the word *christos* means anointed.[249] Being the Son of God means that he is distinct in his relationship with God.[250] The basic question for readers, then and now, is: Who is Jesus? He cannot just be a mere man as some would have asserted[251] and some still do. His humanity and divinity came together so as to provide the fitting sacrifice to meet the demands of our holy God and the needs of men and women in relation to redemption. He was truly born of Mary but that is not where his journey began. It began in eternity.

The use of the present tense participle *pisteuōn* means that these statements of belief are not made in passing but as one's personal conviction. They are not only statements made but also statements governing one's life. They go deeper than intellectual assent, to include having faith, trust, and commitment.[252] They carry with them not "mere affirmation or passive acceptance of a point of doctrine" but "an active participation in and experience of the person in whom belief exists; not simply belief in the fact but the person himself."[253] Our answer as to who Jesus is will definitely influence how we relate to him and to God. How we relate to God is also closely knit with the way we relate to each other.[254] This is why John knits this matter of

---

249. Peter, in company of John the apostle, declared, "Salvation is found in no one else, for there is no other name under heaven given to men by which we must be saved" (Acts 4:12). Jesus alone is God anointed for salvation.

250. As Jesus made claim of his special relationship with God as Father, in John 16:33, he said, "I (emphatic) have overcome the world" (*egō nenikēka ton kosmon*). Relationship with him provides the needed strength to be overcomers also.

251. The Jews, in Matt 13:55–56 (cf. Mark 3:32), asked several questions (isn't this the carpenter's son? isn't his mother Mary? etc.) in a manner (in the Greek, the questions are introduced with *ouch or ouchi*) that they meant to assert that he was just one of them, an ordinary man.

252. Hobbs 1983: 118–19.

253. Thomas 2004: 241.

254. When my wife serves, let us say, rice, meat, and cabbage, she places each of the

belief to love as he says in 5:1b "the one who loves the one who has begotten (that is God) also loves[255] the one who has been begotten" (5:1). The one who has been begotten can be Jesus[256] or the believer,[257] or both.[258] The point is built on the fact that Jesus is the only begotten Son of the Father (4:9 and 5:18) with John using it "to argue that all who come to faith in Christ are also children of the Father to be likewise loved."[259]

Love in this portion is tied to another deed, namely, "overcome." He says that the one who loves the one who begats also loves (*agapa*) the one who has been begotten (5:1) and the one who has been begotten of God overcomes (*nika*) the world (5:4). Both verbs are in present tense, which carries the idea of a continual habit. These verbs do not have just the strength of making a statement but give a command, even if by implication.[260] They are not just statements of hope but statements of expectation.

---

three in its corner on the plate. As I begin to eat them, I mix all the three and at times she looks at my plate and seems to say, "Not again!" My usual response is "the three will mix in my stomach anyway." John in this section seems to mix the relationship between God, Jesus Christ, and the believer together. The three are his concern. Jesus is the object of our faith; God, together with his only begotten Son, are the object of our love, and we as believers are the beneficiaries.

255. It is not all clear whether we here have a declarative indicative (simply stating what happens) or cohortative one (stating what ought to happen). If the first, then John is making the statement so as to build a case on it, for example, we believers are a family. If the latter, then he is continuing his exhortation to his readers to keep on doing the expected, that is, loving each other. The declarative sense probably fits better within this context, but it also implies the cohortative. If in general practice one who loves a parent also loves the parent's children, then that practice should also apply in the spiritual context. To love God and not his Son Jesus Christ, and the believers as his children, would be abnormal.

256. While there seems to be very few (if any) commentators who would limit this to Jesus, there are several that see the application of the statement here to possibly include Jesus also. For example, Burge 1996: 192; Houlden 1973: 123; and Lieu 1991: 200.

257. Hobbs 1983: 119; Kysar 1986: 104; Kruse 2000: 171; Thomas 2004: 242; Yarbrough 2008: 270; and Painter 2003: 292.

258. The one begotten, and object of love also, can refer to Jesus as he is described in 4:9 as the only begotten Son and also another believer, as the next verse (5:2) continues to say, that "we love the children of God." The statement is a general truth John is stating, for it to be applied within context. In this context, it applies both to Jesus as well as to the believer, who are both qualified to be described as begotten.

259. Jobes 2014: 208.

260. Though *agapa* and *nika* are in the indicative mood, they may rightly be taken as cohortative indicatives.

The Final Test (5:1–5)

The one who has been born of God must see his or her duty as to love God's people[261] and overcome the world.

The issue of love ties closely the love of God and the love for the believer. One cannot love God and not love the believer (5:1). In fact one of the proofs that we love "the children of God" (*ta tekna tou theou*, 5:2) is by loving God. He says that we know we love the children of God "whenever we love God and do his commandments." The love in question here does not just end with the principle of "humanitarian grounds." It is deeper than that. It is rooted in the nature of God who is himself love. It is a love that does not stop when its object becomes stubborn but persistently continues, on the basis of the need of its recipient. This is the distinct difference between what John is teaching here and the naturally kind heart. A naturally kind heart helps but can eventually get tired and stop helping. A heart moved by *agapē* love, which God is its source loves the enemy and wishes him or her well (Matt 5:44). There is here, therefore, the need to love God first so that we will truly and lastingly love others.

John defines the way we love God as keeping his commandments. He says, "for this is love of God (*tou theou*) that we keep[262] his commandments" (5:3a). The genitive *tou theou* is best taken as objective genitive here. It is the love we have for God. Keeping his commandments is the indicator that we love him. Not keeping his commandments is a pointer that we do not love him, even if we make that claim by way of our mouths. Concerning these commandments, John says they are "light, not heavy" (5:3b). The implication of this is that it is not a burden any of us cannot bear. It is within our abilities as we depend on God.

The one who is born of God does not only practice the love of this nature but also overcomes the world (5:4a). Just as "keeping his commandments" is the proof of our love for God (5:3), "our faith" is the means of our victory over the world (5:4). In other words, "we love him and obey him; also we stick with him and overcome the world." The world here is used of the system that pulls us away from God. Our faith in God helps us to climb the mountains and go down the valleys in victory. The worldly system,

---

261. While the focus for John when he talks of those begotten of God at the human level is the believer, this does not exclude the rest of God's creation. It includes all other human beings as God's creation and the principle extends to the environment in which we live. God made everything we see and he said it was all good. Keeping it all good is a duty from God.

262. We here have a present tense (*tērōmen*) and therefore the act of keeping God's commandments in view here is one's continuous way of life.

however, of which the chief designer is Satan, wants to pull us backward so that instead of increasing in love we begin to hate, instead of deepening our belief in the claims of Scripture, we begin to question them. We have come to believe in the claim of Scripture that Jesus is the Christ, he died for us, and by his work on the cross we are able to be born into the family of God. Our duty is to love and to overcome. There is no greater service that our world, in the twenty-first century, needs more than this. Everywhere, there is enmity and not friendship, lust and not love. Many believers have chosen to identify more with the world than with God. The world's way is to kill and not to give one's life for the other; it is to seek for self no matter the means and not to render sacrificial service. May the call of John here be heeded by more and more of us who have been born of God. That is the only hope the world is left with, before Christ brings to an end this age and ushers in his eternal kingdom.

THE UNDISPUTABLE EVIDENCE (5:6–12)

> (5:6) This is the one who came through water and blood, Jesus Christ; not in the water only but in the water and in the blood; and the Spirit is the one bearing witness, because the Spirit is truth (7) Because three are the witness bearers, (8) the Spirit and the water and the blood, and the three are into the one (agreed). (9) If we receive (accept) the witness of men, the witness of God is greater, because this is the testimony of God, that he has borne witness concerning his Son. (10) The one who believes in the Son of God has the witness in himself;[263] the one who does not believe God has made him a liar, because he has not believed in the testimony which God has borne witness to concerning his Son (11) and this is the witness, that God has given eternal life to us, and this life is in his Son. (12) The one who has the Son has (the) life; the one who does not have the Son of God does not have (the) life.

---

263. There is a textual variation here, with some manuscripts reading *autō* rather than *heautō* which we find in the United Bible Societies Greek New Testament. The reflexive use (himself), though more difficult to interpret, is not unfitting in the context. The one who believes benefits self. Exercise of faith and the blessings that go with it is not communal but each person on his/her own.

The Undisputable Evidence (5:6–12)

The focus of this passage is "the witness of God" (*he martyria tou theou*[264]) whose central person is Jesus, referred to as "Jesus Christ"[265] (*Iesous Christos*, 5:6) and as "his Son" (*ho hyios autou*, 5:9, 10) and its substance is that God has made eternal life[266] available to us through Jesus Christ, his Son. John says, "and this is the witness, that God has given to us eternal life" (5:11a) to which he adds, "and this life is in his Son" (5:11b).

The importance for believing this witness is brought out from two angles. First, it is our common practice to believe the witness of men ("if we accept the witness of men,"[267] 5:9a) and God's witness is greater than the witness of men (5:9b). It logically follows that we should be able to accept the greater witness since we do accept the lesser. Secondly, not accepting it has serious implications, namely, the one who does not believe it makes God a liar. John says, "the one who does not believe God (*ho mē pisteuon tō theō*[268]) has made him a liar, because he has not believed in the testimony which God has borne witness to," 5:10). There is nothing more serious than alleging that God is a liar. The act of making God a liar is a tendential act. It is the allegation implied in not accepting his witness, but it is not a reality since God does not and cannot lie.

The possession of this life is conditioned on one thing, namely, "having the Son." John says, "the one who has the Son has the life; the one who does not have the Son of God does not have the life" (5:12). The phrase "to have" (*echein*) here has the idea of believing in him as personal Savior. Earlier (5:10) John says, "the one who believes in the Son of God has the witness in him" (5:10). The point is that eternal life is the possession of those who have believed in Jesus. They do not wait for the life to be theirs in

---

264. The genitive *tou theou* here is subjective. It is the witness God himself has given. The phrase *he martyria tou theou* (the witness of God) is used twice in this passage (both in 5:9) in addition to the phrase *tēn martyrian hēn memartyrēken ho theos* (the witness which God has borne witness to) in 5:10.

265. Each of the two names, Jesus and Christ, has its theological significance. Jesus means "Savior" and Christ means "anointed."

266. The term "eternal life" means a life of fellowship with God, in addition to the fact of lasting forever.

267. In the Greek, we here have a first class condition, equivalent to "since we accept the witness of men," which is something we do often, in our law court and even in our dealings with each other in ordinary life.

268. We here have *pisteuō* and the dative *tō theō*, serving as direct object. The point is, therefore, not believing in God as it is believing what God says is true. The concept of "believing into" is used of our relationship with his Son, with the word "to have" (*echein*) capturing that idea (5:12).

the future but it is already in them. They already bear the stamp of a people who have fellowship with God eternally.

The fact that Jesus Christ has this important function does not only rest on the reliability of God's witness but also the testimony of three things tied to Jesus. The "this" (*houtos*) in 5:6 points back to the end of 5:5 where Jesus is referred to as "the Son of God"[269] (*ho hyios tou theou*). John then adds that "this is the one who came[270] through water and blood" (5:6a) to which he further adds (probably for emphasis) "not in (by) the water only but in the water and in the blood" (5:6b). To these two John mentions a third one as he says, "those bearing witness are three, the Spirit and the water and the blood" (5:7, 8). John brings in the nature of the Spirit as true to further emphasize the truthfulness of the fact that Jesus has this role in God's kingdom. He says, "and the Spirit is the one bearing witness, because the Spirit is the truth" (5:6c). The Spirit is singled out because while "water" and "blood" are things, the Spirit is a Person. Also, as will be shown below, while "water" and "blood" testify by implication, the Spirit bears witness verbally. The three witnesses are in agreement, establishing the matter without doubt. John says, "and the three are into one" (5:8).[271]

While the fact is clear that the three, "water," "blood," and "Spirit," serve as witnesses to the person and work of Jesus as Son of God and Savior of the world, what exact events in his life John has in mind is not that clear. It is quite reasonable, however, that "the water" points to Jesus' baptism by John the Baptist, "the blood" to the cross where he died and shed blood for forgiveness of sin, and the Spirit to either the incarnation by which he became one of us but without sin, or the declaration during the time of baptism. In any case, given that we are many years removed from the original readers' context, differences of opinion must be allowed.[272] The position

---

269. Of course, in addition to the referent of "this" at the beginning of 5:6 being clear from 5:5, he is also mentioned by name in 5:6.

270. The act of coming here (*elthōn*, aorist participle) is not to be understood as entrance into the sphere of humankind (inceptive aorist idea) but his entire stay with us (constative aorist idea) so as to accomplish the mission of redemption. As Marshall puts it, John "is thinking of the total act of his (Jesus') coming into the world" (1978: 231).

271. The Greek has "*eis to hen eisin*," the neuter *hen* (one) serving as accusative of termination, with focus on goal, end, purpose. The three end at the same point. That is, affirming that Jesus is the Christ.

272. Views are varied. For example, just to mention some, "water" and "blood" make reference to the two things that came out of Jesus' side after the piercing (John 19:34–35), the sacraments of baptism and Lord's supper, and the historical events of baptism and crucifixion of Jesus, among others. Views concerning the spirit as a third witness is that

The Undisputable Evidence (5:6–12)

that will be taken here, without any dogmatism, is that the references are to the water of Jesus' baptism, the blood on the cross, and the declaration following baptism.[273] Relating all of them to events in the life of Jesus makes good sense for he is the focus of the passage.

The baptism of Jesus is recorded in Matt 3:13–17; Mark 1:9–11; and Luke 3:21–22. None tells us specifically why Jesus had to be baptized but it is clear that it was an act of identification with us, human beings. The comment in Luke, "when all the people were being baptized, Jesus was baptized too" (3:21a, TNIV) is enlightening. Matthew records Jesus' response to John's initial refusal to baptize Jesus as "it is proper for us to do this to fulfill all righteousness" (3:15). In God's design, the only suitable sacrifice for atonement needed to be one that was "human" in every way. Jesus was exactly that, and as such he identified with his fellow human beings, though with no sin of his own. By getting into the water like everyone else, he demonstrated his oneness with us.

The three Synoptics record the Holy Spirit making the declaration that Jesus is God's beloved Son.[274] In 1 John 5:8 where the three testimony bearers are listed together, the Spirit is mentioned first, for it is the clearest statement on who Jesus is.

The crucifixion of Jesus is recorded in Matt 27:32–56; Mark 15:21–41; Luke 23:26–49; and John 19:16–37. In John's account we read, "one of the soldiers pierced Jesus' side with a spear, bringing a sudden flow of blood and water" (19:33). It is the blood that has been given theological significance in the New Testament (1 John 1:9; Acts 20:28; Col 1:20; Heb 13:12; 1 Pet 1:19) and therefore it is reasonable to view the flow of it here as the item bearing witness in 1 John 5:6–8.

Not withstanding the need not to be dogmatic, therefore, there is good reason to view John as saying that God's witness that Jesus is the way provided for our salvation finds testimony in the events of Jesus' baptism, declaration following baptism, and the provision of blood on the cross.

---

it is the Person of the Holy Spirit and as said above, the declarations the Holy Spirit made about Jesus. For a critical analysis of these and other views, see Smalley 1984: 277–84. Also Brooke 1912: 132–36; Brown 1982: 581–85; and Lieu 2008: 208–14.

273. See also Painter 2003: 302–8; and Yarbrough 2008: 282–83; among others.

274. Matt 3:17: *houtos estin ho hyios mou ho agapētos*; Mark 1:11: *su ei ho hyios mou ho agapētos*; and Luke 3:22: *su ei hyios mou ho agapetos*. The translation: "This is my beloved Son" for Matthew, and "You are my beloved Son" for both Mark and Luke. Whether addressed to the people around Jesus (Matthew) or addressed to Jesus directly (Mark and Luke) the declaration of who Jesus is, is clear. He is God's Son.

With the mention of these three witnesses, the matter is laid to rest. There is no debate about it. It is God's way and no other way for salvation and attainment of eternal life. For the faithful ones (*tekna tou theou*, children of God) this serves to affirm their position. It is, therefore, not only from a testimony more reliable than the witnesses of men they accept in every day life, but it also meets the threshold of what is required, namely, two or three witnesses (Deut 17:6). As for those who are denying that Jesus is the Christ, their case is thrown out. It has no basis on which it can be trusted in a fair court of law.

The Ultimate Reward—Eternal Life (5:13–21)

(5:13) These things I wrote[275] to you in order that you may know that you have eternal life, to those who believe in the name of the Son of God (14) And this is the boldness which we have before him that if we ask something according to his will he hears us. (15) And if we know that he hears us whatever we ask, we know that we have the things which we have requested[276] from him. (16) If someone should see his brother sinning (committing) a sin (which is) not to death, he will ask (should ask[277]) and he will give to him life, to those sinning not to death. There is a sin to death; I do not say that he should ask concerning that one. (17) Every wickedness is sin, and there is sin not to death. (18) We know that everyone who has been born of God does not sin, but the one who has been born of God, he keeps him and the evil one does not touch him. (19) We know that we are of God and the whole world lies in the evil one (20) And we know that the Son of God has come and has given to us understanding in order that we might know (*ginōskōmen*) the true one, and we are in the true one, in his Son Jesus Christ. This is the true God and eternal life. (21) Little children, guard yourselves from the idols.

---

275. This translates an aorist verb, *egrapsa* which can also be translated "I write" (taking it as epistolary aorist), "I wrote" (taking it as constative), "I have written" (taking it as resultative).

276. The literal translation here would be "we have the requested things which we requested." The use of both the noun (*ta aitēmata*) and the verb (*ētēkamen*) are probably for emphasis.

277. The indicative here may be treated as having the force of imperative, taking it as volitive future.

The Ultimate Reward—Eternal Life (5:13–21)

Just as John includes, toward the close of his gospel, the purpose for writing it (John 20:31) he now provides to the readers the purpose for writing this letter. He says, *tauta egrapsa humin hina eidēte hoti zōēn echete aiōnion* (5:13). Though the aorist *egrapsa* may be treated as epistolary here and so translate it as "I write to you" or "I am writing to you"[278] (see notes 98, 274, and also index on shades) it may even be better to translate it as constative or resultative—covering the purpose for writing chapters 1:1–5:12,[279] which he now plans to bring to a close. This allows for the translation, "these things I wrote to you (or have written[280] to you) in order that you might know that you have eternal life" and without excluding what follows here since it forms the conclusion of the "these things." The goal of 1 John, then, is for the readers to know that they have eternal life. As said earlier (see note 128) the phrase "eternal life" combines both quality and quantity of life, with the former taking prominence. It is life of fellowship with God, and it cannot be terminated for it lasts forever. The adjective "eternal" (*aiōnion*) is placed last in the Greek construction (the verb *echete* ["you have"] separating it from *zōēn* ["life"]) for emphasis. It is a life that, as Paul says (using "love of Christ") in Rom 8:35–39, cannot be brought to an end by life circumstances or even the wish of the devil.

This quality of life is given "to those who believe in the name of the Son of God" (5:13b: *tois pisteuousin eis to onoma tou hyiou theou*). Though salvation is a free gift, there must be the willingness to receive it. It is those who put their faith in Jesus who receive it. The double genitive *tou hyiou*[281] (of the Son) qualifying "the name," and *tou theou*[282] (of God) qualifying "the Son" is important. Those who want to just claim that they believe in God and assume they have this life are mistaken. This faith is in the name of God's Son, and his name is Jesus Christ. There is no way one can believe in the Scriptures, and in this verse in particular, and leave out Jesus as the object of saving faith, for life eternal.

---

278. Haas et al. 1972: 124; Jackman, 1988: 157; Grayston 1984: 140; Brown 1988: 120; and Kistemaker 1986: 359; among others.

279. Brooke (1912: 142) limits this to 5:1–12 because of its focus on Jesus Christ as the object of faith.

280. Bruce 1970: 122; and Burdick 1985: 384.

281. Here is a qualitative genitive. There are many names people may invoke but it is that of the Son which has been given this function.

282. Here is a genitive of relationship. There is the one Son who has special relationship with God. John has, in this epistle, been defending that this is Jesus Christ.

It is usually a life of fellowship with God and therefore a life of boldness. Fear is cast out as John had said in 4:18. In this boldness, as between a parent and an obedient child, we are able to approach God and "whatever we ask[283] according to his will[284] he hears[285] us" (5:14). What a privilege this is! Since God owns the whole universe, all we cannot ask him and get is what is not in his will. This is why our prayers should always include admission that his will be done. So long as we sincerely leave room for that, we can ask God for anything even when it looks like we are crazy in the eyes of the world. Is it healing we need? Is it school fees we need? Is it means of transport (sometimes a big challenge for the average minister of the Gospel in some places) we need? Is it a wife or husband we need? No wonder James told his readers, "You do not have because you do not ask God" (Jas 4:2a) and Jesus exhorted, "Ask and it will be given to you, seek and you will find, knock and the door will be opened to you" (Matt 7:7). What a joy and relief! All we need is to be in his will and ask what we need as we allow the same will to govern the situation.

As if the assurance carried by "he hears us" (*akouei hēmōn*[286]) is not enough, John goes on to say, "if we know[287] (*oidamen*) he hears us whatever we ask, we know that we have the things we have requested from him" (5:15). The verb "we have" (*echomen*) is an interesting one here. One would expect John to use the future *exomen* (we will have) but he uses the present tense. It deliberately stresses the certainty of the provision.[288] By

---

283. The thought here is, "whatever we ask" and "whenever we ask" (iterative present). There are moments when we are not asking but appreciating the provision of what we have asked.

284. This captures the manner in which we ask and also the purpose for which we ask it. We need to ask in faith and with God's glory (which includes meeting our needs [not wants] and the needs of others) in view.

285. Here is a gnomic present. It is a guaranteed outcome of our asking so long as the condition "according to his will" has been met. There is never a moment that our asking falls on deaf ears. Our God never slumbers.

286. Here we have a genitive of direct object, as *akouō* is one of the verbs that take genitive for direct object. The hearing is deeper than mere registering of the words we have spoken. It here means, he answers us.

287. Here we have a third-class condition (the condition of probability). While God hearing us is guaranteed, our conducting our lives as people who know that as a fact is not guaranteed. There are many times we live lives of doubt rather than of faith. When we grasp and apply this knowledge, we are able to live as children who have all they need even before we have the things in our hands.

288. We here have a futuristic present.

The Ultimate Reward—Eternal Life (5:13–21)

implication, we need to ask and then begin to thank God as if we have it already. No wonder Jesus warned about using too many words as if God hears only when we babble (Matt 6:7, TNIV: "And when you pray, do not keep on babbling like pagans, for they think they will be heard because of their many words"). An example of babbling is "Lord, I need a pair of shoes; yes, Lord—shoe number eight, Oh Jesus—one that does not hurt my foot; and Master Lord—a brown one will be best." Instead, our prayer should be, "Lord, I need a pair of shoes and I thank you for I know I will receive the best for me, from you."

For a reason John does not tell us, he uses the example of a brother who has sinned to communicate the impact of praying the kind of prayer he has here. The promise is that God will give what we ask. The application used here is a brother "sinning a sin not to death" (*hamartanonta hamartian mē pros*[289] *thanaton*, 5:16). While the sin in question here is not clear, resulting in different views,[290] the effect of the prayer is very clear. John says

---

289. The preposition *pros* with the accusative, as we have here, has the idea of movement toward. So, the translation "sin not leading to death" is quite appropriate. The sinner is moving that direction.

290. While there is no view on this matter that solves all the problems, there are three primary paths that seem possible: (a) to identify the sin unto death as unbelief which goes with the failure to confess Jesus as the Christ (see for example, Hobbs 1983: 139; Kysar 1986: 114; Jobes 2014: 236; Painter 2003: 317; Kruse 2000: 192; Kistemaker 1986: 363; Jackman 1988: 164; Grayston 1984: 144; and Brooke 1912: 146). This sin is done by unbelievers only (Jobes 2014: 236) and within the context of the epistle, more so by the secessionists. This position is left to answer why John uses "brother" (*adelphos*) for one doing such a sin (with a possible solution offered being that this is a person who is among believers but actually not a believer) and also how such a person is doing sin unto death while he/she never left the sphere of death to enter the sphere of life. A possible solution offered is that "unto death" means, the outcome of the sin in view (unbelief) is death and not that there is movement from sphere of life toward the sphere of death. (b) To understand the reference as specific sins, by believers, that are not forgivable. Tradition has placed on this list such sins as murder, idolatry, apostasy, and adultery, while quoting Matt 12:31 (cf. Mark 3:28–30 and Luke 12:10) to add blasphemy on this list also (see for example, Yarbrough 2008: 310–11). This view is left to answer the question whether a believer can sin so much that he/she loses salvation. In other words, are there sins that are excluded from God's promise to forgive as stated in 1 John 1:9? (c) To view the sin unto death as adamant refusal, by a believer, to respond positively to God's invitation to live a holy life, followed by God's act of cutting short the person's earthly life. This view takes death here to be physical, and it goes with the view that the sin is deliberate and persistent, making the sinner practically immune to God's invitation to repent. This is left with the question of whether a believer can do such sin in view of 1 John 3:6, 9. A possible solution is to view 1 John 3:6 in light of John's emphatic demarcation between light and darkness and take "is not able" as equivalent to "is not consistent with," and "cannot" of

that the one who sees[291] should ask (*aitesei*[292]), and he[293] will give[294] to him (the sinning one) life (5:16a). By implication, God will hear the prayer. The sinner whose sin is not unto death will confess, be restored and continue to live. Life in this context is taken to be in contrast to physical death though it is not the majority view.[295] At times, continual sin by a believer results in God cutting short the life of the believer. This seems to be what was

---

3:9, as meant to say God will not allow it. In other words, this is to be understood not in terms of what one who is born of God has potential for but in terms of God's permission to do it. God terminates the physical life of such a person without the person losing his/her status as child of God. Viewed from this perspective, sin not unto death takes the route of act of sin → conviction of the Holy Spirit → confession → restoration, while sin unto death's route is act of sin → conviction of the Holy Spirit → dismissal of the conviction → hardening of heart and persistence in sin → physical life termination but no loss of salvation. This leaves both sins to be understood as done by a fellow believer as the use of "brother" (*adelphos*) seems to demand.

291. John expresses this using a third class condition (*ean tis idē*). This means that not everyone in a congregation will see (the sense of sight removing the issue from a rumour or some gossip) but since no person lives in an island of his or her own, another believer may get to know the matter for sure.

292. Though this can be rendered "will ask" (predictive future), it carries more weight than that. It is imperative in nature (volitive future). It is what John is saying we should do when we qualify to be the *tis* (someone) here. We must never leave a dying brother to perish in sin. That would not be an act of love, which is at the center of this epistle.

293. The Greek has a third-person singular verb, *dōsei*, without a clear expression of its subject. Most commentators take this to refer to God, since they also see the life in question to be spiritual life. However, If one takes "life" here to mean physical life (as opposed to spiritual death) the person who asks (he will give him) or the act of praying (it will give him) fits in quite well, and avoids importing God as subject from 5:13–15. The one who prays is credited as giving the life but without taking the glory that belongs to God. God is credited with honoring (hearing) the prayer of the praying brother.

294. Within the context of the view taken in this work (that we have physical death and physical life here) the act of "giving" does not mean the sinning brother did not have life before. The years added, after the prayer is answered, is what is in view. The oncoming physical death is cancelled and by implication, this is life given.

295. Most commentators are of the view that John has in mind here spiritual death, not physical death (See Schnackenburg 1992: 249; Kruse 2000: 192; Burge 1996: 215; Kistemaker 1986: 363; and Plummer 1888: 123) with the primary argument being that John does not, in the epistle, use "death" or "life" in the physical sense but only in the spiritual sense. There is, however, nothing within the immediate context against taking the physical death and physical life position here. It is a possible position (Thomas 2004: 269; Painter 2003: 315; and Bruce 1970: 124) even if not the first choice for most commentators. In such Old Testament passages as Num 18:22; Deut 22:20–25; and Isa 22:14, physical death was used as punishment for certain sins. The same is also implied in the Qumran literature, for example 1QS 5:11–13 and 8:22—9:2.

The Ultimate Reward—Eternal Life (5:13-21)

happening in Corinth where some were taking the Lord's Supper casually (1 Cor 11:30[296]). The situation John has in mind here, therefore, could be one in which a brother is continuing in sin (the participle *hamartanonta* is in present tense) exposing himself to his earthly life being cut short by God. When the brother who sees this and prays for the sinning brother's confession and restoration, and the prayer is granted (as the context is one of promise that God hears), the restored brother is given life (more years to live).

There is a brother who is in continual sin but is struggling to get out of it, and there is a brother who is in continual sin and has reached the point of even mocking the art of prayer (equivalent to grieving the Holy Spirit). John says that he is not talking of the mocker but about prayer for the one who is really struggling to get out. John's words are: "There is a sin to death. I do not say that he should ask concerning that one" (5:16b). The one to be prayed for is the one "sinning not to death" (5:16a). The struggling one will be restored on basis of our prayers, but the mocker's life will be cut short. This underlines the importance of prayer for persons whom we know love God but for one reason or another have become the slaves of a particular vice. It may be a brother or a sister. We should never cease to pray for them—to be restored before they reach the point of their lives being cut short. Usually, when we counsel with people who are in sin, we can sense whether theirs is a struggle or there is a mockery of the way of salvation. When John says, "every wickedness is sin, and there is sin not to death" (5:17), he is probably saying that both the struggling brother and the mocker are involved in wickedness[297] but there is hope for the one who is simply struggling.

In this letter, therefore, there are different levels in which sin is looked at:

1. There is the level of sinlessness, which should be the goal of the one who has been born of God (1 John 2:1a). This is why John writes on the subject. It is the apex of spiritual growth.

---

296. 1 Cor 11:30: "That is why many among you are weak and sick, and a number of you have fallen asleep." God punishes sin, at times by withdrawing from the body good health, with the climax being physical death.

297. The Greek construction is *pasa adikia hamartia estin* which can be translated either as "every wickedness is sin" or "every sin is wickedness."

2. There is the level of falling in one act of sin. The provision for Jesus' advocacy is promised (1 John 2:1b). It is the reality for all of us until glorification.

3. There is the level of continual sin but with hope of restoration (5:16a). This is for the struggling brother/sister. He or she senses the need to overcome but is defeated. Prayer for such brother or sister is needed.

4. There is the level of sin with no hope for restoration (5:16b). This leads to life being cut short. He or she knows the need to overcome but has become so hardened that he or she begins to mock it. There is no hope for this one. Prayer for such is a waste of time, and so John says that the prayer he is talking about is not for such.

5. There is the level of continual sin and without sensing failure within. This is not for those who have been born of God (1 John 3:6, 9; 5:18a). It is not possible for those who have been born of God not to sense failure because God's seed is in them. It would be like one who appears to be alive and does not feel when hot iron bar is placed on him or her. When there is continued sinning as if nothing is happening, this becomes a possible pointer that there was no spiritual birth, to begin with.

The first four levels have to do with a believer and the fifth relates to an unbeliever. When John says, "we know that everyone who has been born of God does not sin" (5:18a) he is talking of sinning as we find in level five above. When John continues and says, "the one who has been born of God, he (God) keeps and the evil one does not touch him" (5:18b), he is talking about eternal security and applies to levels one through four. Even the worst of the levels dealing with a believer (level four), God still keeps such a one, but by way of cutting his or her life short. God's purpose for his creation is that it would glorify him. When it does not, he does not deny it as his creation. Everyone who has been born anew is God's new creation, to glorify his name here on earth. When he or she ceases to glorify God, God calls them home. They have no ministry here on earth, any more. They are given "early retirement" for spiritual health reasons.

Lest this assurance of eternal security for the believer, whether in levels one, two, three, or four, becomes sufficient comfort, John finishes with a reminder of who we are and an exhortation of how we will relate with anything that draws us away from attaining the ideal (level one above), namely the idols.

The Ultimate Reward—Eternal Life (5:13-21)

We are:

1. God's Servants. He says, "we know we are of God" (*oidamen hoti ek tou theou esmen*,[298] 5:19a). The term "servant" is used here because of the Greek preposition *ek*. We do not just belong to God but that is where we proceed from. This is to be evident whether we are looking at our approach to politics, money, status, or anything else we are involved in, in this world. God's perspective forms our worldview. We always look at things from that worldview. We are here to glorify him: nothing more, nothing less. In contrast to who we are, "the whole world lies in the evil one" (*kai ho kosmos holos en tō ponērō keitai*,[299] 5:19b). Between us and the world, there is bound to be tension, since we are "of God" and the whole world "lies in the evil one." The believer is meant to be the "ruling party," showing God's justice and righteousness. When these are not noticeable any more, it means the believers have failed in their duty and have allowed the evil one to take charge. One can judge for oneself how good or poor job we are doing as believers!

2. A people with knowledge of the true God. John says, "and we know (*oidamen*) that the Son of God has come, and has given to us understanding in order that we may know (*ginōskōmen*) the true one" (5:20a). John's use of the two words for knowing (*oida* and *ginōskō*) makes it clear that even though there is some overlap, *ginōskō* goes beyond some mental learning to a heart relationship. The statement "this is the true God" (*houtos estin ho alēthinos theos*) in 5:20b makes it clear the "true one" in 5:20a means God.

3. A people positioned in the true God. John says, "and we are in the true one" (*kai esmen en tō alēthinō*, 5:20a). We do not have to be moved elsewhere. It would be a movement from the sphere of truth to a sphere of lies. John defines this position as being *en tō hyiō autou Iesou Christō* ("in his Son Jesus Christ," 5:20). Being in this position is not only being "in the true God" but also being in the sphere of eternal life (5:20c).

---

298. The verb "to be," *esmen*, here is a durative present. Our status as being "of God" is neither momentary nor does it end. Once we have been born of God, we attain and continually keep that status.

299. This also is a durative present. It is a permanent fix of the world, in this context standing for the evil system directed by the evil one.

As he draws this conclusion to a close and addresses his readers as "little children" (a title of endearment) John exhorts them, "guard yourselves from the idols" (*phulaxate heauta apo tōn eidōlōn*, 5:21). An idol is anything[300] that would take them from the right position in which they stand, which is the position of being in God and in possession of eternal life. They do not only possess the eternal life but they are also to promote it. An idol may be something that robs my heart or my time from having the fellowship with God that will keep me growing in the position he has placed me—in his Son. We do not need to look for these idols out there, but they can be the very things we like most—even being so busy in service for God that we neglect being in his presence for renewal of our spiritual strength and fellowship with him. We can also be so occupied with our desire to be praised by men, whether in our attainment of good grades or distinction in service, that we neglect what God says about us.

Not the least but very relevant for the context of John's readers are persons who have so occupied a place in our lives that they hinder us from relating to God directly as his children. Within the African traditional practices, for example, there were the ancestors who in some cases were venerated to the point that God became so distant in everyday life that he was almost lost in the people's thinking.[301] The same position seems to be

---

300. Griffith, in his book *Keeping Yourselves from Idols* (2002: 14–27), discusses four perspectives from which an idol can be defined. The four are conceptual, sociohistorical, metaphorical, and literary. The conceptual would define idol in terms of "a referent that has existence only in the mind" like false ideas, false teachings, false beliefs, and the like (2002: 14). The sociohistorical approach views idol within the context of images (physical objects) that would be located in such places as a temple for purpose of worship. This, for example, is what Daniel in Babylon refused to bow to and they were common in the Greco-Roman world. The metaphorical approach explains idol within the context of disobedience to God, equating it with such referents as sin, apostasy, and the like. The fourth approach sees a passage like 1 John 5:13 as a literary device to relate what is taught in the epistle to the idol polemic we find in the Old Testament. Of these four interpretations, Griffith says that the conceptual is more popular among the interpreters of "idols" in 1 John 5:13 (2002: 14). A reflection on what John has discussed in the five chapters as he encourages his readers to live up to the standard God expects from them, the conceptual and the metaphorical stand out as most fitting in this context. Both false teachings about Christ and a life contrary to the nature of God who is light and love are at the center of his exhortations in the letter. They have the potential of taking the readers away from the true God, thus qualifying to be described as potential idols.

301. It is to be noted that many young people, especially in the urban centers in Africa, have no interest in knowing what their African ancestors believed and practiced. However, the principle John lays down here applies to the new philosophies they encounter in the universities in the same manner. Any teaching that takes their faith from

The Ultimate Reward—Eternal Life (5:13–21)

taken by some religious leaders (whether referred to as apostles, prophets, or similar titles) today. Just as John's readers were to make sure the false teachers and their new (opposed to what they had been taught by John and other apostles) but false discoveries did not become their idols, so we also must watch lest anyone comes between us and our personal relationship with God, through his Son Jesus Christ, and faithful study of God's word. May the Lord help us to know (*ginōskein*) and love (*agapan*) him more even as we serve him better!

The choice of the verb "guard" (*phylaxate*) is an interesting one here. It implies that the temptation to be occupied by things or persons that can stand between us and God will be so strong and subtle that we must be alert about it all the time.[302] The use of plural verb also means that even though the focus is each of us individually, we are also to watch as institutions, churches, and even nations. The God who reigns forever asks for allegiance from all his creation. Such statements like "in God we trust" (American inheritance) or "justice be our shield and defender" (a line in Kenyan anthem, and at the center of what God desires among his creation) must permeate all way of life. God competes with nobody and nothing, and nobody is to be given more honor than him. This is a calling for those who have been born of God and desire to have confidence before God as his children.

---

the Sunday school God and Jesus they learned in their tender years is an idol.

302. The verb John uses here, *phylaxate*, is in aorist tense but this does not mean it is a one-time activity. It is a constative aorist, seeing all the efforts put in place and at all times as a whole.

2 JOHN

Translation

(1) The elder, to the chosen lady and to her children, whom I (myself[1]) love in truth, and not I alone but also all who know[2] the truth, (2) because of (on account of) the truth which remains in us,[3] and will be[4] with us[5] forever (3) Grace, mercy, and peace will be with us—from God the Father and from Jesus Christ, the Father's Son, in truth and love.[6]

(4) I rejoice[7] greatly because I have found that some of your children are walking in truth, just as we received a commandment from the Father. (5) And now I urge you, lady, not as writing a new commandment to you, but (as one) which we have had[8] from beginning, that we love one another (6) and this is love, that we walk according to his commandments; this is the commandment, just as you heard from him, that in it you should walk. (7) Because many deceivers have gone[9] out into the world, those who do not confess Jesus Christ coming[10] in the flesh; this is the liar and the antichrist (8) Watch yourselves in order that you might not lose

1. There is an emphatic *egō* here.
2. Taking the perfect tense verb here (*egnōkotes*) as intensive in shade.
3. Dative of sphere.
4. Taking *estai* as a predictive future.
5. Taking the genitive here as genitive of association.
6. "Truth" and "love" are datives of sphere, showing where grace, mercy, and peace will be in operation.
7. The verb in the Greek here (*echarēn*) is in aorist tense but has been taken as a dramatic aorist, thus the present tense translation in the English. It is a feeling caused by what John has found out about this congregation.
8. We here have the imperfect *eichomen*, taken as durative imperfect. It is the same idea we have in 1 John 2:7 but there using the second person *eichete*.
9. This translates an aorist tense *exelthon*, taken here as resultative.
10. The confession they do not make is the fact that Jesus came in the flesh.

what we worked[11] for but you may receive full reward (9) Everyone who goes beyond and does not remain in the teaching of Christ does not have God; the one who remains in the teaching, (this one[12]) has both[13] the Father and the Son. (10) If anyone comes to you and does not carry this teaching, do not receive him into a house and do not say to him "greetings." (11) for the one who says to him "greetings" has fellowship with his evil works.[14] (12) Although I have many things to write to you I did not intent[15] to do so through paper and ink, but I hope to come to you and to speak face to face, in order that our joy may be made complete. (13) The children of your elect sister greet you.

Commentary

In this letter, we also find the two key issues John deals with in 1 John, namely, the practice of love and the belief about Jesus coming in the flesh. Instead of writing five chapters, however, he writes only one. Also unlike 1 John where the author only implies (by the use of first person pronoun, "we") that he is one of the witnesses of the life and teachings of Jesus Christ, he here identifies himself as "the elder" (*ho presbyteros*[16]).

11. The translation here, as elsewhere in this work, is based on the United Bible Societies Greek New Testament. The variants in the manuscripts are worth noting, especially whether we should read "we have worked for" or "you have worked for."
12. The *houtos* here may seem to be unnecessary in the English, but it serves the purpose of emphasizing the contrast. There is "this one" in contrast to the earlier one.
13. This seems to be a remote meaning of *kai*. While it primarily means "and," "even," and "also," it should not be limited to that. In this context "both" makes better sense.
14. There is the use of article with both the noun and the adjective, for equal emphasis of the two.
15. We here have a deponent passive aorist, *eboulēthēn*. It can be a constative aorist, focusing on when he sat down to begin writing, or epistolary aorist with a possible translation as "I do not purpose" but an aorist used since when his readers receive the letter, the action would be in the past.
16. *Presbyteros* here is a title of some authority (due to experience or age) and honor, not of office in the sense we use "church elder" today. The use of "village elder" in some African contexts may be close to the idea it carries here. It is not a position one is appointed or elected to but an earned title. Within the context of the addressees, the use of the title (without mention of his name) was sufficient. For example, in the local church I attend, people for now refer to me simply as "Professor." So when someone says, "we will ask Professor to pray" everyone knows who is meant. With time, however, later generations (after there are others with the same title) will not know who was meant. We have similar situation with the use of "the elder" here. The original readers would understand

2 JOHN

The chapter (letter) is addressed to "a chosen lady" (*eklektē kuria*) together with "her children" (*tois teknois autēs*). John qualifies the children[17] as persons he loves ("whom I myself love," *hous egō agapō*) and then adds "in truth" (*en alētheia*[18]). John is not alone in this, for he further states, "and not I alone" (*kai ego monos*) and then clarifies, "but also all who know[19] the truth" (*alla kai pantes hoi egnōkotes tēn alētheian*,[20] v. 1). The use of language here, and in v. 13, leaves no doubt that John is writing to a church and the children are its believers.[21]

In the opening verse, therefore, he introduces the themes of love and truth, the very two things that are at the center of his thoughts as he writes this letter. In verse 2 he is even clearer why he is writing. Zeroing on "truth,"

---

that John is meant here. This is not withstanding that, while the position taken here is that it was John the apostle, other views such as a disciple of John the apostle need to be acknowledged (see in the introduction, under "authorship").

17. The pronoun *hous* (whom) is neuter plural, agreeing with "children" in gender and number.

18. The dative here could be dative of sphere, the focus being that the love is expressed within the context of truth (understood by some as "the gospel/revelation of God," Kysar 1986: 124; Kruse 2000: 205; and Jobes 2014: 256; or as "Christ/Lord," Thomas 2004: 41, on basis of his claim to be the truth in John 14:6). It can also be dative of manner, to be translated as "truly," "in sincerity" (Schnackenburg 1992: 279; and Hobbs 1983: 152). In other words, there is no pretense about it.

19. The action of knowing here (using form of *ginōskō*) goes beyond head knowledge to incorporating the truth into the way of life. John uses a perfect participle, with focus on the result (intensive perfect). This is their status. They know the truth.

20. While the use of *alētheia* in the first part of the verse is debated whether it means "truth" in terms of content or "in truth" in terms of manner of loving (see note 18 above), its use in the second part is definitely in terms of the content of the gospel. The extent John has in mind can be limited to Jesus being the Christ and that affecting the way we relate to each other in the exercise of love, or can be more inclusive to include all the fundamentals of the gospel. Even if the focus here is the theme of the letter, it does not need to limit truth to it.

21. This is the position taken by most commentators (for example, Jobes 2014: 255; Yarbrough 2008: 334; Painter 2003: 340; Kruse 2000: 204; Burge 1996: 232; Thomas 2004: 40; Culy 2004: 141; and Kysar 1986: 123) though there are some who take the view that this was a particular woman (for example, Hobbs 1983: 152) and even propose some possible specific names such as Eklecta or Cyria, which are simply the personal names closest to the Greek *eklektē kuria*. The two Greek words, however, are simply the feminine form of *kurios* (lord) with its accompanying adjective for "elect" (*eklektos*) in the feminine form to agree with *kuria*. It is difficult to say for sure how large a congregation it could have been. It could have been one of "a series of small churches distributed over a distance" or communities of about twenty-five believers spread all over the city of Ephesus (Burge 1996: 232).

he says that it is "because of the truth" (*dia tēn alētheian*) which he then describes as "remaining in us" (*tēn menousan*[22] *en hēmin*) and also will be[23] with us forever (*kai meth' hēmon estai eis ton aiōna*). This last description must have been prompted by what he says later; that is, there were persons out there who were teaching contrary to the truth (v. 7). No matter what effort they make to destroy the truth, it will live on.

In his prayer (v. 3) John does not pray only for the chosen lady and her children but also includes himself in it. He also does not make the prayer in the form of a request but affirmation, in the indicative mood. He states what will happen. God the Father and the Lord Jesus Christ will give them (John included) grace, mercy, and peace. His words are: Grace (*charis*), mercy (*eleos*), and peace (*eirēnē*) will be with us (*estai*[24] *meth' hēmon*), and then he states their source as "from God the Father and from Jesus Christ, the Father's Son" (*para 'Iēsou Christou tou hyiou tou patros*[25]). John makes this second statement of affirmation (the first one being that the truth remains forever) to strengthen the chosen lady and her children in standing for the truth. It reflects a context of constant attack from enemies of the truth,

---

22. The idea of truth "remaining in us" may lead to identification of truth as a reference to Jesus Christ or the Holy Spirit (See for example, Burge 1996: 232; and Thomas 2004: 41). However, truth as content of the Gospel remaining is us (in terms of what our convictions are) is not difficult to comprehend and would fit the context better, even as truth is used alongside love in v. 3. Both the noun (*alētheian*, accusative singular, "truth") and the participle *menousan* (feminine, "remaining") have the article. There is, therefore, equal emphasis here. It is the truth remaining in us (dative of sphere) and not another truth.

23. This translates a present tense verb, *estai*, taken here as a predictive future. No opinions of men and women will change or destroy it. Men and women may deviate from it but it persists on.

24. The placing of the verb at the beginning would rightly be understood as bringing in some emphasis. It is equivalent to a promise from God who is faithful in bringing his word to pass. John expresses deep confidence that the three blessings (grace, mercy, and peace) will be their share. See also Kruse 2000: 206. We here have another (see n. 23 above) predictive future.

25. John's stress that the Father and the Son are involved here could almost lead him into the problem of approving nepotism. However, it is a nepotism of blessing others as opposed to the nepotism we see practiced in many societies where family members come together to enrich themselves at the expense of others. The two (*theos patēr* and *'Iēsous Christos ho hyios tou patros*) are the source of the blessings. Specifically, *theou* and *'Iēsou Christou* are genitives of source while *patros* (describing God) and *tou hyiou tou patros* (describing Jesus Christ) identify them further (epexegetical genitives). They are a team together. Anyone who would deny Jesus Christ his rightful place (as the false teachers were doing) would be undermining his relationship with God the Father also.

and in that context calling repeated affirmation from the apostle. Grace helps us to move on during times of discouragement. Mercy facilitates our assurance of acceptance even when we feel like we have failed, and peace keeps our hearts encouraged when we are wrongly attacked. This blessing, however, happens when we are operating within the context of truth and love[26] (v. 3c).

Getting to the situation on the ground, John testifies of what gave him great joy. He says, "I rejoice greatly" (*echarēn lian*) and specifies the cause as "because I have found out that some of your children[27] are walking[28] in truth" (*hoti heurēka*[29] *ek tōn teknōn sou peripatountas en alētheia*). While one hundred percent success is the goal, when some of our spiritual children keep the truth during times of great compromises, that is sufficient basis for rejoicing. John's statement here should encourage those who have some of their children walking right. Joy does not necessarily need to be tied only to "all" walking right.

---

26. The two datives (*alētheia* and *agapē*) are taken here to be datives of sphere. Culy (2004: 143) also says, "It appears to point to the context and circumstances in which grace, mercy, and peace will be experienced: clinging to the truth and loving one another." See also Kruse 2000: 206; and Yarbrough 2008: 337. Dative of means, however, has also been suggested. Kysar (1986: 126), for example, views the two nouns as "the means by which the blessings of grace, mercy, and peace are present among the readers." See also Painter 2003: 344. While means is a possibility, it may be better to work with the dative of sphere since truth and love are the ones that will be developed further in the letter, as if John is saying, "grace, mercy, and peace" will be ours so long as we remain in the truth and practice love.

27. *tōn teknōn* is treated here as genitive of the whole. "Some" is supplied to make sense out of the Greek construction. If John wanted to say that all the children of the chosen lady (that is, everyone in the congregation) were walking in truth, he would have used the nominative case *ta tekna*.

28. This translates a present participle and is taken to be aoristic present (the walking coinciding with the finding out) though it can also be durative present with the idea that it has been and still is their determination to walk in the truth. It has also been taken as an independent participle (functioning here as an indicative) so that the force of *hoti* at the beginning of the phrase is retained.

29. An intensive perfect, focusing on the result and synonymous with "I now know." It could imply that there was some concern in John's mind whether the church was keeping to the truth of the gospel, or it could be that their difficult circumstances necessitated this affirmation. Yarbrough's position (2008: 340; also see Painter 2003: 347) that what John is saying here is that he has encountered some members of the congregation who walk according to the truth implies that he had assumed that everyone had departed from the truth, and that does not seem to be the picture John is painting here.

Commentary

Those walking in truth do so in obedience to a commandment from the highest office. They do it, "just as we received a commandment (*entolēn*) from the Father" (*para tou patros*, v. 4b). John does not, at this stage, state what commandment he has in mind, but as he addresses the (chosen) lady specifically, he sheds some light on this. In v. 5 he says, "and now, I urge you, lady, not as writing a new commandment to you, but (as one) which we have had from beginning,"[30] to which he adds, *hina agapōmen*[31] *allēlous* ("that we love one another," v. 5b). As said above, "lady" makes reference to "a church," and so this love for one another is for all the members of the church.

As if there is ambiguity in what he is saying, he repeats himself but for emphasis. In v. 6a he says, "and this is love, that we walk according to his commandments." The singular, commandment (*entolēn*), in v. 5 is now replaced with the plural (*entolas*) as John defines love as obedience to them. The love here seems to be love for the one who gave us the commandments (plural). The only way we can show out that we love him is by obeying him. Yet love for him does not end there. It causes us to love his people. This is why John then adds, in v. 6b, "this is the commandment (singular) just as you heard from him, that in it[32] you should walk." The point is that the commandment (singular) to love is part of a package (including all his commandments) from God, and obeying that package is what shows that we love God. By the same token, obeying the commandment to love one

---

30. We met the use of "beginning" (*archē*) within a similar context in I John 2:7. The position taken there is that the focus of the "beginning" is within the context of the readers' experience, using 2nd person plural (you). Here, John uses 1st person plural (we), and also attributes its origin to the Father. The focus, therefore, may be the very first expression of such a commandment as we have in Lev 19:18. Since God is love by nature, his relationships center on love and so expected of all who relate to him, whether Old Testament saints, John and other apostles, or his readers.

31. A durative present idea here, equivalent to "we keep on loving one another." It is a life style believers must maintain all the time. It is not a matter we pause to decide whether to do it or not.

32. The "it" (feminine pronoun *autē*) can stand for *agapē* (love), *entolē* (commandment) or *alētheia* (truth), which are all feminine nouns in the Greek, and are found within the immediate context. Since a call to walk (conduct oneself) is a call to obedience, and obedience corresponds well with commandment, the "it" is probably best understood here as referring to "commandment" which is in turn defined as "love." The semantic density view (advocated by E. R. Wendland, and mentioned by Kruse 2000: 208) which argues for the three feminine nouns to be referents of *autē* together is not in agreement with common usage of language where we speak to be understood. The fact that it is not clear to us does not give to us permission to attribute deliberate ambiguity to John.

another is very important since the source of it is God. God is source of the part (act of love) as well as he is source of the whole.[33]

Having brought the issue of practice to a good stage, John turns to the matter of belief. The introduction of it (in v. 7) with *hoti* ("because") means that he sees a connection between the practice and the belief. The connection may be more implied than stated. It could be that the false teachers on the matter of belief will be the same ones who will lead them astray on the matter of practice. If Jesus is not what the believers were taught he is, then why should they listen to what he taught? Also, even as Yarbrough says, the duty of the believer, according to John, is "full-orbed confessional (doctrinal), behavioral (ethical), and relational (devotional) integrity before God."[34] So, from vv. 7 to 11 John pays attention to the deceivers.

John says that they are "many" (*polloi planoi*) and "they have gone into the world" (*exēlthon eis ton kosmon*). Deceivers are usually persons who have previously been informed on something and have come to change their minds about what they were taught. In other words, rarely does a deceiver begin with an empty slate about what they are deceiving on. It would not be surprising that the verb "they have gone out" carries its full force. They were once faithful, at least fellowshipping with them,[35] but have now gone out. The "into the world" location is the opposite of the congregation of the faithful. They are out there, seeking to make the faithful join them. The specific detail of belief John mentions is that "they do not confess Jesus Christ coming in the flesh" (*hoi mē homologountes*[36] *Iesoun Christon*

---

33. Though John focuses on the commandment "to love," he is conscious that God's commandments may be more than that. They are given out of love and they can also be summarized (see for example, Marshall 1978: 68) under love. To respond to them in obedience is also a demonstration of love. A child who tells mom or dad, "I love you," and then disobeys at the same time, has not understood what love is. He/she may have known that it is a statement that makes a parent smile or give in to the child's request (as a mere formula) but that is not love. True love goes with obedience.

34. Yarbrough 2008: 342.

35. Assuming that it is the same group of people John refers to here as deceivers that he refers to as antichrists in 1 John 2:19 (and there is good reason to make that assumption, including that their falsehoods is the same, concerning who Jesus is), in 1 John 2:19 he focuses on where they came from (*ex hēmōn*, from us) and here he focuses on where they went (*eis ton kosmon*, into the world). These are people who once knew the truth but have now departed from it. Such are more dangerous to the truth than persons who never knew of the truth at any time. This is why John at times uses the strongest language possible (for example, vv. 10–11) in warning his readers about associating with them.

36. Here is a present tense, meaning that this is their theological statement of faith.

erchomenon[37] *en sarki*, v. 7b). Literally, this can be rendered as that "they do not confess a coming in the flesh Jesus Christ."[38] They deny his humanity, and they do it as a settled issue in their minds,[39] not that they are wondering about it. John hastens to say, in v. 7c, "this is the liar and the antichrist" (*houtos estin ho planos kai ho antichristos*).[40] John feels so strongly on the matter that he uses the article *ho* ("the") with liar as if he is the only one. In 7a he had said there are many of them, but this one who undermines the nature of the only Savior of the world, is a special one. He is to be pointed out vividly. He is also "the antichrist," that is, the one who undermines Christ and all that he stands for.[41]

John raises an alarm to the chosen lady and her children, "Watch yourselves" (*blepete*[42] *heautous*). In other words, be on guard, each of you

---

37. Though the coming in the flesh had happened decades of years before John wrote, the event is mentioned here using a dramatic (historical) present. John wants his readers to be participants in the event as if they are witnessing the event as they read the letter. It can also be perfective present, to be rendered "has come in the flesh" (cf. 1 John 4:2 where the perfect tense is used) but dramatic present shade is more appropriate for the context. John wants to lay the reality of the event before his readers with some emphasis. Kruse's position that the use of perfect tense in 1 John 4:2 focuses on "Christ's status as one who came in the flesh" while 2 John here (v. 7) focuses on "the process of his coming in the flesh" (2000: 210) captures the idea fairly well though it sounds more like differentiating an intensive (status) and extensive (process) of two verbs that are both in perfect tense. The notion of dramatizing for more effective communication must not be lost. To be noted also is the view (acknowledged [not supported] for example by Thomas [2004: 46]; Stott [1964: 209]; and Brown [1982: 669] among others) that John had the second coming of Christ (*parousia*) in mind (giving the present participle a futuristic shade) but this seems foreign to the context.

38. The participle has an adjectival function, and both the participle and Jesus Christ are in accusative case, telling us the direct object of the verb confess.

39. The act of not confessing is expressed using a present tense.

40. The two predicate nominatives refer to the same figure. He combines deception and being antichrist.

41. Comments on the use of antichrist have been made against 1 John 2:18 (see chapter "1 John," notes 115 and 120 above). It is a title given to someone who is against Christ. Its usage is limited to the first two Epistles of John, and probably builds upon a "general concept of a powerful end-time figure opposed to God" found in Jewish apocalyptic literature (Kruse 2000: 210). The antichrist proper is himself "a superhuman being in opposition to God and his purposes" (Kruse 2000: 211). Human beings preceding him, in the form of false teachers, however, promote what he will do, and so qualify (according to John) to bear the title.

42. Here is a present tense, best taken as durative. The watching is not to leave any moment unprotected, for any gap would give the liars an opportunity to strike. As an imperative, it is better to see it within the context of urgency, equivalent to "look out"

taking care. There is the implication that when one is not on guard, he/she leaves a loophole for this very dangerous wrong belief to enter. It must be blocked out. John gives reason for this urgent plea as "in order that you might not lose what we worked for[43] but you may receive full reward"[44] (*hina mē apolesēte ha eirgasametha alla misthon plērē apolabēte*, v. 8).

Lest anybody would think that John does not have good reason for expressing this with so much urgency, he states a universal truth. In v. 9 he says, "everyone who goes beyond and does not remain in the teachings of Christ does not have God" (*pas ho proagōn kai mē menōn en tē didachē tou christou theon ouk echei*), which he contrasts with "the one who remains in the teaching, this one has both the Father and the Son" (*ho menōn en tē didachē, houtos kai ton patera kai ton hyion echei*).

John here paints two pictures. The first picture is of a person who has two characteristics.[45] He "goes beyond" (*proagōn*[46]) and "does not remain"

(Hobbs 1983: 156) than a command (Lieu 2008: 255). It is more an entreaty than a command. In general, John is happy with the congregation.

43. This implies that John's readers were beneficiaries of his ministry (though there is a variant reading using second-person plural). He has established them in the truth which is now under attack. The statement has nothing to do with losing salvation/eternal life as Jobes (2014: 265), Kruse (2000: 212), Thomas (2004: 47), and others hold. The focus is the ground gained in the walk of fellowship with God, and the depth established in true doctrine or as Yarbrough puts it, "the integrity of their belief and behavior" (2008: 349). John is addressing persons who are in the truth, and so believers in the sense of John 3:16. He, on the other hand, describes those who hold the false teachings as having proven that they were not part of the faithful (1 John 2:18). What the false teachers can do is not change the status of the faithful as believers but as believers who hold the truth firmly.

44. John's desire is that his readers will receive "well done" evaluation from God, with no marks lost. Those who identify "full reward" as eternal life need to make a comment whether eternal life is given in portions. The reward here fits more within the context of 1 Cor 3:10–15 than portions of salvation.

45. The fact that it is one person (whoever it is—the Greek has *pas ho*) in view is supported by a Granville Sharp theory construction. The first participle (*pragōn*) has the article and the second (*mē menōn*) does not; both are in the nominative case and are connected by *kai* (and). The act of remaining has the element of allegiance to. For *pragōn*, see the note below.

46. The lexical meanings of *proagō*, in its intransitive usage are "go before," "lead the way," "precede," "walk ahead of" (Gingrich 1965: 182), or similar ideas. Since John here sees Jesus' teaching as the canon that defines truth, the focal/contextual meaning of the word is to go beyond. It causes us to imagine truth as defined within perimeters that should not be crossed. Those perimeters are the teachings of Scripture. Our speculations on matters that are not clear must be subjected to the authority of Scripture and not vice versa. On matters that the Scriptures are clear, we must accept them as true even when

(*mē menōn*). Both characteristics are expressed using the present tense to say that it is a fixed state or established position.[47] In other words, it is not someone who is lost or in search for the truth. John defines the perimeters beyond which this person goes using the phrase "the teaching of Christ" (*tē didakē tou Christou*). The person goes beyond it, and does not remain in it. This person, John says, "does not have God" (*theon ouk echei*[48]). John seems to be dealing with a situation where someone(s) was choosing the Father over the Son.[49] Within the context of John's readers, the error was a denial of Jesus' humanity (v. 7). This is the basis of his being a suitable Savior for fellow members of humankind, and needing to be defended when under attack. The phrase *hē didakē tou Christou* (the teaching of Christ) may mean what Jesus taught (taking the genitive *tou Christou* as subjective) or what had been taught (to John's readers and also those who were going outside its perimeters) about Christ (genitive of content) by Jesus himself,[50] John, and other apostles, or even someone else. The strength of the genitive of content position is that it includes the specific matter of Jesus' humanity and goes beyond it.[51] The believers John is writing to must have known much more about Jesus than just the fact that he came in the flesh, though that is the focus here.

---

we are not able to comprehend them at the moment. Specifically for John's readers, it amounts to representing Christ "in ways that are inconsistent and irreconcilable with established apostolic recollections that crystallized in Christian congregations over a period of a half century or so" (Yarbrough 2008: 350).

47. The first (*proagōn*) is best taken as a perfective present (the person has gone beyond) and the second (*mē menōn*) as durative present. He/she has established his/her station away from the teaching of Christ.

48. The verb (*echei*), which is also in present tense, is best taken as a gnomic present. It is the guaranteed outcome for the person who has the two qualifications of going beyond and not remaining in the teachings of Christ. The idea of *echei* here is that of having relationship or fellowship with.

49. This is not uncommon today. There are some faiths that in their zeal to protect monotheism deny Jesus his status as God. The Jehovah's witnesses who are very zealous about religion also pass on the heresy that Jesus is only a god (specifically, the first creature out of the hands of the one God; see also chapter "1 John," notes 117 and 118). While the Trinity (three in one) is still difficult to comprehend fully, we do not need to deny it because we cannot express it fully. It is the truth of Scripture.

50. Such utterances of Jesus, as we find in Mark 10:45 for example, are clear statements about his humanity.

51. See also (some using the description "objective genitive" but saying the same thing) Painter 2003: 354; Lieu 2008: 258; and Kysar 1986: 130. For support of subjective genitive, see Hobbs 1983: 157; Schnackenburg 1992: 286; and Thomas 2004: 48.

This first person is thus left empty handed. He/she has given Jesus (as taught by John) away and John also takes away the Father as he categorically says, such person does not have God. As a contrast to the empty-handed person is picture number two. The second picture is of "the one who remains in the teaching" (*ho menōn en tē didachē*). From context, we know that this is "teaching of Christ" just as in picture one. This second person is doubly blessed. He/she does not only have Jesus but also has the Father. The Greek has *houtos kai ton patera kai ton hyion echei* ("this one has both the Father and the Son"). The verb (*echei*) here (also as above) is a gnomic present (it is a guaranteed outcome) and is placed last for emphasis. John is asking those who may want to give some ear to the false teachers, "Do you want to be empty handed or do you want to be doubly blessed?" while at the same time telling the faithful, "Hold first what you have; you are doubly blessed." Yes, for him, it was crucial that the truths about Jesus be held firmly.

Within that spirit, and in view of the importance of the matter, John gives some pastoral guidance for how to deal with the deceivers. He says, in v. 10, "If anyone comes[52] to you (*ei tis erchetai pros humas*) and does not carry[53] this teaching (*kai tautēn tēn didachēn ou pherei*) do not receive him into a house (*mē lambanete auton eis oikian*) and do not say to him 'greetings'" (*kai chairein autō mē legete*). John here gives two prohibitions[54] in dealing with the carriers of this spiritually poisonous teaching. They are not to be welcomed into a house. This mention of a house is because the

---

52. John here uses a first-class conditional, which can be paraphrased as "when someone comes," for it is more probable that someone will come than not get someone at all.

53. The Greek verb *pherei* is in present tense. We can understand this in the sense of one being a carrier/promoter of the teaching than a situation where someone has written down a heretical statement for purpose of asking his/her instructor whether it is correct doctrine.

54. John uses a present imperative with *mē* for both prohibitions (*mē lambanete* and *mē legete*). Working with the traditional understanding of prohibitions (which the present writer here has not been convinced needs to be abandoned unless the context cannot support it; also see chapter "1 John," notes 102, 151, and 183) we have a situation here where some of the false teachers are former friends who have gone out (out of congregation of the faithful and out of the truth as to who Jesus is). While the faithful fellowshipped (in meetings) with them before, that has to stop lest they become party to their false teachings. John is here teaching "excommunication" at the personal level. The promotion of true doctrine is more important than friendship of someone who promotes error. If Jesus gave his life for us, what is giving up a friendship so as to guard the truth about him?

COMMENTARY

believer has control over who enters or not.[55] In a house also is where such a person would be refreshed to carry on his/her mission of poisoning others spiritually. The second prohibition, not to greet, builds on the fact that extending greeting to someone implies some form of fellowship.[56] The point is that such a person is to be avoided by all means.[57] In terms of application to our today's relationships, it is good to note that the prohibition is not on whether to respond when the false teacher greets or not,[58] but is on the believer initiating (*legete*) the greeting. The believer should not, for such an act communicates fellowship, even as John says in v. 10, "for the one who says to him "greetings" has fellowship with his evil works"[59] (*ho legōn gar autō chairein koinōnei*[60] *tois ergois autou tois ponērois*). Again, John's focus here is not to teach impoliteness, but to stress the seriousness of false teaching.

55. While the focus is private house, it can also include where the community of the faithful meet since believers met in their houses for fellowship (Kysar 1986: 131; also Lieu 2008: 259; and Burge 1996: 236).

56. In the local church I attend in Kenya, it is a common practice for men to greet each other by putting shoulders together (at times more than once) and the ladies to give each other a kiss or two on the cheek. What it amounts to is acceptance of each other as believers in the Lord. To extend the same to a promoter of heresy would definitely be unacceptable.

57. This way of handling persons who have the potential of contaminating the community of holiness does not begin with John's instructions here. In the Qumran community, there was a level of departure from the truth that resulted in a member being banished, with the holy ones instructed not to associate with his goods (for example, do business with) or advice on any matter (1QS 8.23). It is the same principle Paul wondered why it had not been applied, by the Corinthian church, to the adulterer in 1 Cor 5.

58. In most cultures of the majority world (and especially in the African context), answering someone else's greeting is a matter of etiquette more than agreement. John is not here teaching us to have bad manners but to beware that we do not give false teachers a refreshing welcome that gives them either the physical or emotional renewal for their next target.

59. While evil works may include immoral deeds in a general sense, the focus is the promotion of wrong teachings about Christ. For John, the divide between who Christ is and how one behaves is very narrow. That is why in this epistle he gives attention to both.

60. The verb *koinōnei* (he fellowships) is an aoristic present. It happens whenever the faithful greets (*legōn* being understood as iterative present) the carrier of false teachings. In other words, greeting such a person coincides with fellowshipping with him or her, together with the evil works they promote. Since darkness and light do not have fellowship, so also their promoters. It is notable that John focuses on fellowshipping with the person's evil works. The person may change but the evil has a fixed state as evil. Helping the carrier promote the evil works would make one a party to what is evil. That, according to John, is not allowed at all.

2 John

In this letter and also in 3 John, John concludes with a statement of having more to say than he says in the letter, but postponing that until an anticipated face-to-face conversation. This is spelled out in v. 12, "Although I have[61] many things to write to you (*polla echōn humin graphein*) I did not intend to do so through paper and ink (*ouk eboulēthēn dia chartou kai melanos*) but I hope to come to you (*alla elpizō genesthai pros humas*) and to speak face-to-face"[62] (*kai stoma pros stoma lalēsai*). It may not be necessary to say that John did not have the time to write. He could have used an amanuensis if necessary. It was probably that there are some issues that were too sensitive to put into writing. As he anticipates the face-to-face talk, he says that when it takes place, it will perfect that joy the elect lady and her sons will experience reading this short letter. He says, "in order that our joy may be made complete" (*hina hē chara hēmōn peplērōmenē hē*). Those who are included are John and the chosen lady and her children, though it may not need to be limited to them. There could be other persons of like mind though not specifically mentioned who may be included in John's use of "our." In 1 John 1:4 he had used the phrase to include all the witness bearers of Jesus' accomplished ministry of redemption.

Just as John began by disguising who the exact recipient is, he also disguises where he is writing from. This was not uncommon when being a believer was, at times, a risky undertaking. He concludes, "the children of your elect sister greets you" (*aspazetai se ta tekna tēs adelphēs sou tēs eklektēs*). Children certainly are believers of a particular local congregation.[63] The carrier of this letter, probably a special confidant of John, had quite a few details to share with the recipients, details we are not privy to. The message, however, is clear, and the warnings as relevant today as they were then.

---

61. This translates a participle (*echōn*) which is taken to function here as concessive. It can also be translated, "Because I have many," taking it as causal.

62. The literal translation of the Greek would be "mouth to mouth" but John is here using a figure of speech (synecdoche) where the mouth (part of face) stands for face. It is also found in the Old Testament, in Num 12:8.

63. Though "certainly" is used here, it must be acknowledged that there are some who would prefer "probably." Lieu, for example, says, "The closing greeting from the children of 'her elect sister' (13) probably indicates that behind both women are two churches with their members (the children)" (2008: 3).

3 JOHN

Translation

(1) The elder, to the beloved Gaius whom I (myself) love in truth[1] (2) Beloved, I pray you prosper and be healthy[2] with reference to all things, just as your soul prospers.[3] (3) For I rejoiced[4] greatly when brothers came and testified[5] of you with regard to the truth,[6] how you are walking[7] in truth. (4) I have no greater joy than these (moments[8]), when[9] I hear my children are

---

1. A dative of sphere. It spells out the context within which the writer (John) expresses this love.

2. Prospering and being in health are infinitives, but with an accusative (*se*) as subject.

3. Durative present. Gaius' soul is showing continual growth, and this is evident from his acts of love. John is asking God that Gaius will also prosper in other matters of life.

4. Constative aorist, simply reporting John's response as he received the good news concerning Gaius' conduct.

5. The verbs "came" and "testified" translate present participles. Their action is simultaneous to the action of the main verb (*echarēn*, I rejoiced). Their translation here as "came" and "testified" is due to attraction by the main verb whose tense is aorist. They can also be taken to be historical present, dramatizing what happened.

6. This translates a dative of reference. Its focus is not that the brothers testified with truthfulness as opposed to lying, but that they testified about Gaius' walk in truth.

7. This captures a current reality (aoristic present) as John wrote this letter. It could also be durative present, to capture that it is Gaius' habitual practice. He walks in truth as his way of life.

8. "Moments" has been supplied here to complete the idea of "these" (*touōn*), which is used in the Greek without an accompanying noun.

9. "When" here translates *hina* (from the Greek). Though its more common use is "in order that" (expressing purpose) or simply "that" (introducing content), it makes better sense here to render it as "when" (a remote meaning) in view of the context. It could also be seen as providing an infinitive function to the verb *akouō* following it (thus, "to hear" (see other possible examples of this in Gingrich 1965: 100).

3 JOHN

walking[10] in the[11] truth. (5) Beloved, you do faithfully whatever you work out for the brothers,[12] and this (even) for strangers, (6) who[13] have borne witness,[14] before the church,[15] concerning you[16] with reference to love,[17] (and) whom you will do[18] well sending[19] on their way in a manner worthy of God; (7) for they went

---

10. "Are walking" here translates a participle (*peripatounta*) taken here as used independent of a main verb, with the function of an indicative.

11. The use of the article with truth (*tē alētheia*) makes allowance for the fact that "truth" (see also vv. 3, 8, and 12) is wider than the exact one Gaius is walking according to (note the *anarphoric* use in vv. 1 and 3b).

12. "The brothers" are the accusative of termination, with focus on the beneficiaries of Gaius' good deeds. John, however, adds even another group, that is "strangers." What this seems to communicate is that Gaius' loyalty to the truth was such that he did well in serving both those he knew and those he did not know, so long as they were promoters of truth.

13. The "who" (*hoi*) here could refer back to both the brothers and strangers. However, given that the strangers are the ones who were on the move, and consequently talked about Gaius' acts of love elsewhere, they are the more specific group John has in mind here.

14. The act of "bearing witness" here translates an aorist in the Greek. It is translated as "have borne witness," taking it here as resultative aorist. The recipients of Gaius' acts of love have already spread this reputation.

15. The "church" here is broader than a local congregation. It refers to any gathering these strangers have ended at, as ministers of the truth. Local churches who preach the truth are part of a larger church. It is the larger church John has in mind here.

16. The genitive here (*sou*) is taken as genitive of respect/reference. It is with respect to (concerning) Gaius, they give report.

17. This translates a dative (*tē agapē*) and is a dative of reference. It narrows the report on Gaius to the specific virtue that he exhibits and is of interest to John here. It is on the matter of love, specifically.

18. This may be best taken as a progressive future. Its focus is the future opportunities that will avail themselves to Gaius. Just as he has been doing, as a matter of way of life, he will do well to continue with the same practice when the opportunities come his way in the future. In other words, John commends Gaius for his past deeds and encourages him to keep it up.

19. This translates a participle (*propempsas*), which may be viewed here as conditional in function. Gaius will be doing well if he sends them on their way in a manner worthy of God (no matter what others may think). However, given that John is encouraging Gaius to do what has already been his practice, it may be better to view it as temporal in function, thus "when you send them on their way."

TRANSLATION

forth[20] on behalf of the name,[21] taking nothing from the Gentiles (8) We (ourselves) therefore ought to entertain such persons[22] in order that we may become[23] co-workers in the truth.[24] (9) I wrote something to the church, but Diotrephes, the one who loves to be first among them,[25] does not receive us[26] (10) Therefore, when[27] I come, I will remember[28] his[29] works which he does, with evil

---

20. While "they went forth" is the correct translation (the verb is an aorist), this event is still future in view of the exhortation to Gaius to serve them well in days ahead when the opportunity arises. The idea could be rendered as "they will have gone forth" (proleptic aorist) for the sake of the Name.

21. The Name here is that of God, in view of the preceding phrase (manner worthy of God), but it also includes all that has to do with his mission in Christ Jesus. There is no relationship with the Father except through the Son whom he sent.

22. That is, persons who have gone out on behalf of the Name of God and have refused to receive gifts from the Gentiles so that the truth of the Gospel they proclaim will not be compromised.

23. This ("we may become," *ginōmetha*) is best viewed as iterative present. It does not deny that "we" (which includes John, Gaius, and others like him) are already co-workers. Its point, however, is that whenever we entertain such persons (whether in the past, the present, or the future), we become (or continue to be) co-workers.

24. The focus of "the truth" (a dative, *tē alētheia*, in the Greek) is the sphere in which the co-working will take place. It is within the context of promoting truth, that is, the message that such persons are out to propagate.

25. "Them" is the bigger group of which Diotrephes is one person. It (*autōn*) is therefore a genitive of the whole. Who it refers to is not specified, but from context, it includes those in leadership capacity (elders) of the local congregation Diotrephes belonged to.

26. The pronoun "us" (*hēmas*) here includes John and all others who are out to proclaim the truth. It is quite possible that John had written requesting that the local church, in which Diotrephes was one of the leaders, stands (most likely in a matter that would appeal to the members' hospitality) with John and others in the team promoting the truth, but Diotrephes was not for the idea.

27. The Greek here can be literally translated "if I come" (a third class condition) but the indefiniteness seems to be on when it will happen and not whether it will happen. Verse 14 is clear that John's plan to go there was not in doubt.

28. "I will remember" (*hypomnēsō*) is a predictive future. This is what John plans to do.

29. The genitive here (*autou*) is subjective genitive. Diotrephes is the doer of the deeds in question. The function of what follows, then ("which he does"), is for emphasis.

3 John

words[30] accusing us unjustly, and as if not satisfied[31] with these, he himself[32] does not receive the brothers and those who desire to do so, he prevents and puts them out[33] of the church. (11) Do not imitate bad thing but the good one. The one who does good is of God; the one who does evil[34] has not seen God.[35] (12) Concerning Demetrius,[36] witness has been borne by all and by the truth itself; and we also bear witness, and you know that our testimony is true. (13) I had[37] many things to write to you, but I do not wish[38] to

---

30. The dative here (*logois ponērois*) can be related to the preceding ("which he does using evil words," dative of means) or with the following ("with evil words accusing us unjustly," dative of manner in which the accusations are made). The latter position (dative of manner) makes the allegation more serious. The accusations are not only unjust but are also expressed using evil words (language). With dative of means, the words could qualify as evil on basis of being unjust, but with dative of manner, the words have two distinct qualities: they are unjust and they are evil. Dative of manner is preferred here in view of the plural "these" (*toutois*) in the following phrase. In other words, there are already more than one wrong deed before John adds a third (and even a fourth) one.

31. This renders a participle (*arkoumenos*) which in this context is modal in function. He adds more evil deeds as if what he has done already is not enough.

32. The use of *autos* here is not just to provide the subject of the action (the subject is already clear in the verb *epidechetai*) but also to bring out emphasis. Diotrephes was worse than a lion who after eating and is very full sits beside the remaining carcass of the victim animal to prevent another lion from eating it. Lions rarely do this, and one wonders whether animals, at times, have better love for each other than some human beings have for others!

33. All the verbs used to describe Diotrephes's actions here are in the present tense. They are his usual responses whenever (iterative present) there is need, and situations arise calling for a love response. He does not want to get involved, he forbids others from getting involved, and if they do so he punishes them with excommunication.

34. Both "doing good" and "doing evil" are presented in the present tense. It is a pattern of life that is in view but not a one-time deed.

35. Taking the perfect tense here as intensive. Such a person does not have the life changing effect the sight of God would bring.

36. Demetrius is in dative case in the Greek, and is taken here to be dative of reference. That is, "as for Demetrius."

37. This translates an imperfect tense (*eichon*) which would literally be, "I was having," with focus probably on when he began writing. We do not know what triggered his change of mind and instead of writing decided that the matters would be talked about face-to-face. A possibility is that as he wrote, something came up and made it possible or necessary for either John or Gaius to make a trip to where the other person was.

38. This is best taken as an aoristic present, "I do not now wish to write." If what caused the change of strategy was something that came up as he wrote, this would also have caused a change of his wish. Initially he wanted to write more than we have, but with what we do not know (John does not tell us) coming up, he now does not wish to do so.

write to you by means of ink and pen (14) but I am hoping[39] to see you before long, and we will talk face to face.[40] (15) Peace to you; the friends greet you. Greet the friends by name.[41]

COMMENTARY

Apart from John the author, the third Epistle of John lays before the reader three persons. There are Gaius the lover of brothers, and even strangers; Diotrephes the self-promoting leader lacking love for others; and Demetrius the person of good reputation. Apart from a phrase of the author's introduction (v. 1a) and some concluding remarks in vv. 13–15, the one chapter of 15 verses, can be examined around these three persons as follows:

Gaius	vv. 1–8
Diotrephes	vv. 9–11
Demetrius	v. 12

From each of the three persons, there are lessons we can learn for our benefit and the benefit of the church of Christ. Our examination of the passage will, therefore, be focused on what John says to, or about, each of the three persons.

---

39. This is another aoristic present, "I now hope."

40. The Greek has *stoma pros stoma* (literally, "mouth to mouth") but this is a figure of speech (*synecdoche*) with the mouth (part of the face) used to stand for the whole (face).

41. What we have in the Greek here is *kat' onoma*. Taking *onoma* as adverbial accusative whose focus is manner, what John tells Gaius here is that he should greet everyone individually. It should not be a collective greeting but a personalized one. This reflects the kind of relationship John must have had with the congregation to which Gaius belonged.

3 JOHN

Gaius (vv. 1–8)

After introducing himself as "the elder"[42] (*ho presbyteros*), addressing Gaius[43] as "beloved"[44] and expressing good wishes[45] to him, John goes on to list the things that endear Gaius to him. John portrays Gaius as:

1. Joy bringer. In v. 3, John says, "I rejoiced[46] greatly" (*echarēn . . . lian*) and introduces it with a *gar* ("for"). The most logical conclusion from the context is to explain the *gar* in view of what John says in vv. 1 and 2. Verses 1 and 2 give the outcome of the rejoicing while vv. 3 and 4 give the basis for the rejoicing. The outcome is endearment (shown by calling Gaius beloved and describing him as the one he loves) while wishing him prosperity[47] and good health,[48] and the basis is that Gaius is walking in truth (v. 3). John is not guessing about Gaius' walk in the truth. He says that brothers came and testified about it (v. 3). John

---

42. This is the same way the writer introduces himself in 2 John (see comments there).

43. We find a person called Gaius elsewhere, in Acts 19:20 (a companion of Paul), 1 Cor 1:14 (one of two persons Paul baptized), and Rom 16:23 (mentioned as host of Paul). Whether any two (or more) of these mentions refer to the same person is difficult to say.

44. John uses the vocative *agapēte* (beloved) in v. 2 and repeats it in vv. 5 and 11. He also attaches the description "the beloved" (*tō agapētō*) to Gaius' name as he identifies the reader of the epistle (v. 1) and even describes Gaius as "whom I love in truth" (*hon egō agapō en alētheia*) in v. 1b.

45. The good wish is expressed in form of prayer. John prays that Gaius will prosper and be in good health not just in matters of the soul (spiritual matters) but also in all things. John does not specify what is included in all things, but we can be sure it includes material blessings. Gaius did not spare his material possessions to extend hospitality to others who had committed their lives to the promotion of the truth, and it would be very natural for John to ask God that he replenishes what Gaius spent on others. The Lord always extends his generosity to those who are generous.

46. John is not saying that "he rejoiced" and he is not rejoicing. He is reporting what happened (constative aorist) at the point when brothers brought report how Gaius was doing in the area of walking in truth.

47. First, John acknowledges that Gaius is prospering in spiritual matters (*kathōs euodoutai* [durative present] *sou hē psychē*, 2b) and then wishes Gaius prosperity beyond just spiritual matters (*peri pantōn*, v. 2a). When spiritual people prosper in political, economic, social, and such other areas, they become a blessing to the church and society in general. They become God's servants in ministering to the needs of his people. It, however (as history has shown), calls for deliberate attention to the spiritual sphere, otherwise it often becomes crowded out by economic and social successes.

48. While there should not be partiality in ministry, we cannot deny that there are some of those we minister to who give us a special feeling of joy. It is a natural outcome and not partiality.

then in v. 4 provides a general principle concerning himself and the truth. When he hears that his children are walking in the truth, it gives him greater joy than any other moment. That is how close John's heart is to the truth. It is closer to his heart even than Gaius' health and material prosperity.[49]

John's use of truth (*alētheia*) in this letter seems to be both comprehensive (covering all that he would judge to be correct doctrine) and specific, in the case of Gaius having the focus on hospitality. When the articular is used (for example, vv. 3a, 4b, 8, and 12) it seems to be referring to truth in general, no matter what issue of belief or practice, while the anarthrous use (for example vv. 1 and 3b) seems to restrict truth to a particular issue. In this epistle, the focus where truth is tested is in the area of hospitality, practiced by Gaius but prohibited by Diotrephes. Gaius' walk in it caused John great joy.

2. Faithful worker. Repeating again his address of Gaius as "beloved," John in v. 5a says, "you do faithfully whatever you work out" (*piston poieis ho ean ergasē*). As other qualities (below) will show, Gaius was not a lazy person. He was not the kind of person who folds his/her hands so as not to get involved. He was active. The main point here, however, is that he was faithful in what he did.[50] It is a common observation that some of us would prefer not to work if we had a choice, and even more serious is that since we must work (no one wants to pay us for sleeping or partying) most of us work only to the level of pleasing our masters but not governed by the principle of faithfulness.[51] The Greek word *pistos* can be translated "trustworthy, faithful, dependable."[52] While "faithful" is the translation chosen for

---

49. This is the difference between the prosperity John is talking about here and most of the versions of prosperity gospel in our day. Today's prosperity gospel focuses on God multiplying our money, our cows, and healing every disease and often neglects the spiritual aspect of the listeners' lives. John's first focus is the spiritual (the truth) and then the other areas of life follow after that.

50. The Greek uses a present tense "you do" (*poieis*), best taken here as iterative present. Whenever the opportunity to do something arose, Gaius was faithful at it.

51. I have observed in many occasions, within an African local context, workers who covered weeds with soil (as opposed to uprooting it) so well that their employers paid them their full salary, convinced that a good job had been done, just for the same weeds to sprout out when the rains came. Those are unfaithful workers. Gaius was a model of a faithful worker in what he did. The principle can be applied to any occupation the Lord calls us into.

52. Gingrich 1965: 173.

it in this context, the other English adjectives are also applicable. One who is faithful can also be trusted. He or she can also be depended on. So long as the assignment was under the attention of Gaius, John would be sure that it will be taken care of well.[53] Unfortunately, the world is short of such kind of persons today. Many do not only do their work poorly, they also cannot be trusted with public property. In the African context (and not limited to it), corruption continues to be a challenge due to shortage of faithful workers like Gaius. So, here is another challenge for us who have accepted the truth John was so concerned about. Some countries boast of high percentage of Christians but have very little to show in the area of good ethics. May the Lord help all of us, beginning with me, to be persons who combine hard work and faithfulness!

3. Loving person. John, in 5b, identifies the beneficiaries of Gaius' faithful work as "the brothers, and even strangers" (*eis tous adelphous kai touto xenous*). The Greek word *adelphoi* needs to be understood as inclusive of both male and female persons who are our relatives in Christ. It is everyone who belongs to the family of God, the family of faith. Someone can be a brother or sister in the Lord because we worship together or we live in the same estate, but there are also brothers and sisters in the Lord whom we have never seen or even heard of before. They are strangers to us. Gaius provided his service to both the known persons and those he did not know of before, so long as they were related together in the truth of the message he believed in. It takes more grace to help the persons we do not know than to help the person we know. Gaius had even that higher grace.

Those whom Gaius has extended his service of hospitality to have spoken of it in public,[54] and they see it as acts of love on the part of Gaius. John describes them (especially the strangers, who would be on the move) in v. 6 as persons "who have borne witness, before the

---

53. If John, as an apostle, was the one allocating funds to be used in providing hospitality (and there was no such funds then, but some churches today do have them), he would never hesitate giving to Gaius any amount, for each cent would be used for what it was meant for.

54. Just as it happens today, and it was the practice in the time of Paul as we see in Acts 14:26–27, so also it appears to have been toward the end of the first century when John wrote this epistle. One who had gone out as a missionary would share with his/her local church (most of them, household churches) how the Lord prospered their way, and those the Lord used to do so.

Gaius (vv. 1–8)

church, concerning you with reference to love" (*hoi emartyrēsan sou tē agapē enōpion ekklēsias*). Gaius may have done it privately, but the recipients shared it publicly (before the church). We cannot underestimate what effect, to the glory of God, an act of kindness we did to someone in need can have. Even when done at the material level, it can bring much fruit at the spiritual level. Gaius helped materially but his recipients saw him as a model of love. Sharing the gospel is not just by opening our mouths but also opening our hearts and our hands.

After commending Gaius for what he has done already, he encourages him to keep it up. In v. 6b, he says, "whom you will do well sending on their way in a manner worthy of God" (*hous kalōs poiēseis propempsas axiōs tou theou*). The "whom" refers to others of the same kind (people proclaiming the truth and in need of hospitality) or the same but in a future occasion. The phrase "worthy of God" is asking Gaius to place his eyes beyond the persons needing hospitality and attend to them as if he is attending to God. As human beings, which Gaius was also, doing good can, at times, be very tiring. However, when the focus is on God, one can do well without getting tired (for none of us can outdo God). When we focus on God's servants as men and women (and some can even be ungrateful) we soon begin to complain that it is becoming too much.

4. Co-worker. The term "co-worker" (*synergos*) is used in v. 8b where John gives the reason why entertainment is the way of the faithful. The whole clause states, "in order that we may become coworkers in the truth" (*hina synergoi ginōmetha tē alētheia*). At the first level, the coworkers are those entertaining and those entertained. They are partners in promoting the truth. There is, however, a second level that should not be missed. In v. 7 John says that those who are recipients of the entertainment have gone out on behalf of the name (*hyper gar tou onomatos exēlthon*), presumably the name of God in view of mention of him at the end of v. 7. There is a chain of three circles here: the entertained, the entertainer, and God, whose will permeates the activities of the other two. Gaius, therefore, is a coworker with those he entertains as they proclaim the truth and also coworker with God. This is a higher perspective of the ministry of hospitality to preachers of the gospel. We partner with them, and consequently partner with God.

To underline the significance of the ministry of partnering, in matters of hospitality, with those who have gone out to proclaim the truth, John describes their circumstances, in v. 7b, as "taking nothing from the Gentiles" (*mēden lambanontes apo tōn ethnikōn*). "Gentiles" is used here to refer to those who are not in the church. They are not persons of the faith. It is not that they were not generous persons, but they did not care about some of the things that mattered to persons of the truth. Dedication of items for use in everyday life to idols was a common way of life for those who were not persons of the truth (faith). So as to avoid compromising the truth to such Gentile practices, the preachers of the gospel also avoided their items. This made it even more important that people like Gaius and John (the "we" of v. 8 includes such persons) took entertainment of those who had gone out to preach as a very important ministry. John uses the words, "we ought to entertain such persons" (*opheilomen hupolambanein tous toioutous*). This is because if the believers did not do it, the preachers of the gospel would either compromise the truth of the gospel (by taking items of necessity from the Gentiles) or not go out at all.

These four qualities may not be all the characteristics of Gaius, but they are part of what made Gaius a person John would send an epistle to. He needed to be affirmed in what he was doing. In the same place (could be the same local congregation or general area for common leadership to be shared), there was another person called Diotrephes whose qualities are the opposite of what Gaius was.

Diotrephes (vv. 9–11)

Unlike Gaius who was joy-giver, faithful worker, loving person, and co-worker, Diotrephes[55] was:

1. A joy-taker. Instead of giving joy to John and others who love the truth of the gospel, Diotrephes took it away. John describes him as one

---

55. Diotrephes is found only here in the New Testament, and therefore all we can use in identifying him is what John says here. From what is said, he must have had some considerable (if not the top) authority in the church John wrote to. In v. 9, John says, "I wrote something to the church" (*egrapsa ti tē ekklēsia*) and then within that context introduces Diotrephes, and also in v. 10b, he is presented as one who had powers to excommunicate others. He was definitely a person of high standing, with a lot to say when it came to deciding issues.

who "does not receive us" (*ouk epidechetai hēmas*, v. 9b) and "with evil words accusing us unjustly"[56] (*logois ponērois phlyarōn hēmas*, v. 10b). The "us" here are those who stand for and proclaim the truth like John, including John himself. The actions of Diotrephes are presented in the present tense, taken here to be iterative present, and therefore reflecting a fixed way of life. It was not a one-time rejection or one-time unjust accusation, but a repeated practice on basis of a fixed opinion.

One wonders how such a person could have been a leader in the church, but we just need to look around us in the twenty-first century to get an answer to this. There are many, even in church leadership, who allow matters of personal opinion to cause walls of separation rather than make sure the truth of the gospel is always a bridge to reach each other no matter how diverse the personal opinions may be. The gospel is one, and it should always unite us.

John does not see it as a concluded matter. It is a matter he is determined to correct. In v. 10a he says, "Therefore, when I come, I will remember his works which he does" (*dia touto, ean elthō, hypomnēsō autou ta erga ha poiei*). The act of remembering implies that he will bring it up and deal with it. John, as an apostle, had authority over Diotrephes and the wrong must be addressed. We do not know what specific action John had in mind, but we can assume that it was an action appropriate to the damage Diotrephes was causing. When God entrusts us with authority, he expects us to exercise it so as to safeguard the truth. This, at times, is not the case in the twenty-first century church because of fear of persons. Here is another challenge we should pick from the study of 3 John. There are many who have been allowed to continue in leadership when actually they should be asked to step aside. This has led to the church not being the light it should be.

The call for discipline is necessitated by disobedience to be what we should be. We are called to be a team, giving each other the joy of

---

56. The act of "bad-mouthing" (Culy 2004: 164) someone perceived to be an opponent is not unique to Diotrephes who saw John as his competitor worthy of conquering. It is a common feature, even within church circles today, to note persons who have nothing positive to say about their competitors even to the point of twisting what they have said to mean something quite different as a way of presenting false accusations. We do not know for certain Diotrephes' bone of contention against John (for some views, see Burge 1996: 246–48). After pointing out that we are not able to draw a definite conclusion whether there was doctrinal matters or it was all on church administration, Burge says, "Diotrephes was simply a powerful lay leader who had gained control and rejected John's authority" (Burge 1996: 248).

a united victory in our proclamation of truth. This is what Diotrephes failed in. Instead of causing joy for John (and others) he caused pain, taking away John's joy and by extension the joy of others he could have ministered to.

2. Self-centered person. Unlike Gaius whom John says was a faithful worker, Diotrephes was a self-centered person. John describes him as "one who loves to be first among them" (*ho philoprōteuōn autōn*, v. 9). Desire to be first here is used in a negative sense. It is not a positive ambition but a proud assertion of one's opinion despite the ideas others may have. The "them" is not specified but the context is clear that it is a bigger group of which Diotrephes, as leader, is one person (see chapter "3 John," note 55). Since Diotrephes placed himself one place in front of every other leader, it meant that when it came to those who were led (other members), he placed himself two seats ahead of them. That is not biblical leadership (leading by example but not dictatorship, washing feet of others but not demanding they wash ours). Also, given that God's servant is called to be faithful in not just taking care of material things but also the flock entrusted to him/her (1 Pet 5:2), Diotrephes did not pass the test of faithfulness. He was too self-centered for him to be faithful like Gaius was.

3. Not a loving person. Unlike Gaius who earns the right to be referred to as a loving person by the brothers (v. 6) because of his acts of hospitality, Diotrephes is described by John, in v. 10c, as one who does not receive the brothers (*oute autos epidechetai tous adelphous*, "neither does he receive the brothers"). This is expressed using a present tense (*epidechetai*). Diotrephes has made it his position on matters of hospitality, that he will not do it—even though it was "widely esteemed and encouraged throughout the ancient world as a moral virtue."[57] John qualifies this attitude with the words, "and as if not satisfied with these" (*kai mē arkoumenos epi toutois*, v. 10b), with the "these" referring to the matters Diotrephes is already guilt of: He loves to be first, he refuses to accept even John, he makes unjust accusations, and uses evil words (vv. 9, 10a). John is indirectly saying, "How negative can he really be? He has exceeded the imaginable level of failure!" Yet, the degree of failure is not ended. John then adds to the list, the failure to receive others.

---

57. Fitzgerald 2000: 522.

4. A loner. Unlike Gaius who was coworker with the brothers (and even strangers) whose business was to proclaim the truth, and ultimately coworker with God, Diotrephes does not only not receive the brothers (see above) but also does not want anybody else to do so. John says that when some want to entertain brothers, Diotrephes "prevents" (*kōlyei*) them, and if they do not follow his instructions not to do so he "puts them out of the church" (*ek tēs ekklēsias ekballei*). Both verbs, "prevents" and "puts out," are also in present tense, spelling out Diotrephes's actions as based on a fixed opinion on his part. This kind of spirit is worse than that of unbelievers. Many unbelievers may not exercise hospitality, but they will not stand in the way if someone else does it. One possible explanation could be that Diotrephes saw other believers' involvement in the lives of the brothers who are out to proclaim the truth as depriving the local church of resources and consequently his source of income.[58] If this was the scenario, then Diotrephes is not alone in this great failure. There are some pastors today who are envious of their members supporting ministries other than those of their local church and under their control. While members need to support the ministries of their local churches faithfully, the support of those who would be in the same position as these brothers (for example, evangelists, missionaries, and others like these) also needs to come from believers in local churches somewhere. The basis for providing support is whether the minister or ministry is done on behalf of the name of God (v. 7).

In view of the damage someone like Diotrephes can cause, John gives Gaius (the recipient of the epistle, and after using the title "beloved" a third time [vv. 1, 5, 11] in this short epistle) a specific prohibition, an exhortation, and its theological basis, all in v. 11. The prohibition and the exhortation are in one sentence: "Do not imitate the bad thing but the good one." Though John does not say "do not imitate the bad person,"[59] Diotrephes must have been in his mind.

---

58. We do not want to do too much psychoanalysis here since John does not tell us why Diotrephes would not want others to do good to others. However, for persons who desire to be first, as it was the case with Diotrephes, there is always the motivating factor of "if I can't (or will not) do it, no one else should—lest they get more praise than I." This is another possible cause for this strange behavior in the life of Diotrephes.

59. John uses the neuter (*to kakon* and *to agathon*) in the first clause and changes to masculine (*ho agathopoiōn* and *ho kakopoiōn*) in the second. He is so "loving" that he does not use the adjective "bad" (*kakos*) for a person like Diotrephes!

He loves to be first; he makes unjust accusations; he uses evil words; he refuses to show love to anybody; he excommunicates those who show hospitality to others, and much more. John exhorts Gaius not to imitate any of these, but to keep on imitating what is good.[60] In other words, John is telling Gaius never to be influenced by someone like Diotrephes, even if Diotrephes may have "stronger muscles."[61]

John gives a theological basis for this, so that Gaius has strong grounds for keeping on holding to the values he treasures. He tells him, "the one who does good is of God" (*ho agathopoiōn ek tou theou estin*[62]) and "the one who does evil has not seen God" (*ho kakopoiōn ouch heōraken ton theon*). John uses the same idea in 1 John 3:16, where he adds also, "has not known him" (God). The seeing is deeper than having an object pass in front and so casually setting sight on it. It has the sense of being overwhelmed by the nature of what has been seen. No one who sees God, as Isaiah saw him in Isa 6:1, remains the same. There is an experience of being overwhelmed by God's glory that follows. One cannot experience this and continue to do evil. Hospitality belongs to the sphere of "good" while lack of it belongs to the sphere of evil.

---

60. Though the prohibition here (*mē mimou*) is expressed using *mē* and present imperative (see also chapter "1 John," notes 102, 151, 183, and chapter "2 John," note 54) there is nothing in the context to warrant a conclusion that Gaius (who is addressed as "beloved" throughout the letter) was imitating anything bad, and therefore this is an exception to the traditional position that *mē* with present imperative has the idea of stopping an action in progress (which is the case in the majority of places). The context must always be given first consideration. Imitating the good thing (*mimou* is expected to serve both the prohibition and the exhortation) is to be Gaius' way of life.

61. At times, it becomes very tempting to join others, not on basis of the values they have, but on basis of their power or numbers. More and more we are seeing politicians, and even church leaders, predict win or loss of motions on the basis of tyranny of numbers. Where have the Christians gone, who can cast their votes on basis of a critical evaluation of issues or on basis of values? John exhorts Gaius to be one of the exceptions.

62. The present tense verb here, *estin*, is best taken as gnomic present. This is a fixed matter in a God-given ethical system. The phrase is frequent in 1 John (3:10; 4:1, 2, 7) and from context (together with the context of similar phrases like "you are of God" [*humeis ek tou theou este*, 4:4] and "we are of God" [*ek tou theou esmen*, 5:19]) it is clear that the focus is the worldview from which one operates. It begins with being born of God, and as a result adopting the practice of God's family. The point here is that doing what is good is God's way. So, as Gaius does what is good, he is doing what is God's will.

Demetrius (v. 12)

John introduces Demetrius into the context without preparing us as readers for what purpose he needs to mention him here. The issue, however, must have been well known to Gaius, the original reader of the letter. From context, it may not be far from the truth to say that he may have been one of the victims of Diotrephes's treatment of other members. John is speaking in his defense, whatever the issue may have been.[63]

John calls into the courtroom three witnesses, in favor of Demetrius: "all," "the truth itself," and "we." In this verse (12) he says, "Concerning Demetrius, witness has been borne (*Dēmētriō memartyrētai*) by all (*hupo pantōn*) and by the truth itself (*kai hypo autē tēs alētheias*) and we also bear witness (*kai hēmeis de martyroumen*)." If the accuser was Diotrephes, as proposed above, the "all" would exclude him but include everyone else who knows of Demetrius's faithfulness to the truth (whether in general or on the specific matter of love to the brothers John has focused on in the cases of both Gaius and Diotrephes). Instead of calling God as one of the witnesses, since he knows all things, John calls truth itself. Truth is an interesting party to be called upon, but as the Kiswahili saying goes, "*ukweli huachi njia*" (truth never misses the way). In v. 10, John had mentioned Diotrephes's unjust accusations leveled against him and those of like mind. With the possibility that Diotrephes has another one against Demetrius here, no matter how loud Diotrephes shouts to make the unjust accusation, what is the truth on the matter remains. No shouting can change the truth into a lie. It is not clear whether the third party, "we," includes John and Gaius alone or is even wider than that. In any case, when John says, "and you know that our testimony is true" (*kai oidas hoti hē martyria hēmōn alēthēs estin*), he is appealing to a knowledge that Gaius was most likely part of.

It is not specifically stated but imagining that Demetrius would add strength to the view of Gaius on matters of hospitality, and Diotrephes was working on undermining that, John is telling Gaius: "Trust in Demetrius and take him as an important party to your view on the matters. His acceptable position on the truth is beyond dispute because it is established by three witnesses."

The scenario here reminds us that church politics is not a new thing. When they arise, however, the important question is, on whose side are

---

63. There is also the possibility that Demetrius was the one who needed Gaius's hospitality and so John was writing to recommend him. He could also possibly have been the bearer of the letter but we cannot be dogmatic about it.

we? Is it on the side of the truth and our position for the glory of the name of God? Answering this question always helps us to avoid serving our own interests as Diotrephes is said to have been doing. More persons like Gaius and Demetrius are needed by the church of the twenty-first century as it deals with its own issues, and serves as light to the society at large.

Concluding Remarks and Final Greetings (vv. 13–15)

As John brings this letter to Gaius to a close, he makes a remark in vv. 13 and 14, which explains why the epistle is as short as it is. It is not that he can't say more, as he says, "I had many things to write to you" (*polla eichon grapsai soi*, v. 13a), but because he expects to see him before long and then they can talk face to face (*elpizō de eutheōs se idein, kai stoma pros stoma lalēsomen*, v. 14). When he says, "but I do not wish to write to you by means of ink and pen" (*all' ou thelō dia melanos kai kalamou soi graphein*, v. 13b), John could be saying that since he will see Gaius soon, those matters can wait as they are not that urgent or he could be saying that they are too sensitive to include them in the epistle. Whatever the case may be, the statement reflects a close relationship between John and Gaius as they seek ways of making sure the truth continues to prosper in Gaius's local area. They can discuss both general issues and also confidential matters.

In the final greetings, John prays that peace (*shalom*) will be Gaius' experience (v. 15a). He certainly needed it, given that he had such persons as Diotrephes in his ministry circles. Peace is that state of heart and mind which enables one to get full sleep after he/she has been accused wrongly. Its focus is not the emotions as much as it is the assurance that God is in control. People like Gaius (and there are many in the church of Christ) need to keep on reminding themselves that the church is not theirs but Christ's (Matt 16:18). When we do so, it minimizes frustration and we can have real peace.

The greeting to Gaius from friends, and to friends from John (v. 15b) shows that they had common friends. It could also be a summary of all those who guard the truth as John and Gaius do. When Jesus had an opportunity to spell out who his real relatives are, he said that they were those who desire to do the will of God (Matt 12:50). It could also be true for John. His friends could be everyone who loves the truth, even as Gaius does.

Concluding Remarks and Final Greetings

When Gaius greets them, however, John asks that he does so by name (*kat' onoma*[64]). Each of them, on his/her own, is important to John.

---

64. *Kat' onoma* is an adverbial accusative whose focus is manner. What John tells Gaius here is that he should greet the believers individually (see also chapter "3 John," note 41). Collective greetings are okay but personalized ones are warmer.

Summary and Conclusion

We opened the discussion on the teaching of these three epistles by raising the matter of quality over quantity. The kind of life John clearly teaches to be the mark of a believer (one who has been born of God) is one that is governed by the nature of God who is light and love. In relation to the matters of quality and quantity, one can thus ask: how many sins can pass the test of God's nature, and be classified under the sphere of light? What level of hatred passes the test of God being love? The answer to both questions, according to the teachings of John in these epistles, is *none*. In the sphere where God is Father (of family of believers) there is no room for a single sin or the lowest degree of hatred. Accumulation of wealth while using wrong methods (including corruption, grabbing, and other common practices for people of the world) places quantity over quality and is against God's formula for blessedness. A student who gets highest marks after cheating in an examination may seem to shine, but that is only before men. In the eyes of God who sees all things, the attainment of the marks wrongly earned is like grass that withers. There is no blessings of the Lord in it. This principle can be applied in all areas of life—whether political, financial, academic, or any other area people of the world place their glory in. God's children seek to please him first (to love him is to obey his commandments) and trust in him as the source of all blessings. After all, he owns all things for he created them all.

God is therefore calling us to a life of moral purity, firm belief based on who Jesus is to us, and hospitality to those who need our assistance within the context of promoting the truth. For John, big numbers at the expense of true teaching is not God's way. Idols of every kind must be eliminated. This is God's will for us.

If this is so, who can stand before the God of the Bible, and in particular the God of the Epistles of John? Who can say that he/she has no

Summary and Conclusion

blame? John leads us to answer this question with "no one" but then gives hope. Jesus has been provided as *hilamos* (means of appeasing God) and advocate (pleading on our behalf before the Father) when we sin and seek forgiveness.

The message here would, therefore, not be complete without pointing us readers to he who, as John says, "came in the flesh," "gave himself as *hilasmos*," and "sits in heaven as our advocate." The call to holiness (with special attention given in these epistles to the exercise of love) is accompanied by sufficient provision. May the Lord help us to not only understand what John teaches in these letters but also make it a reality in our own lives. As for me personally, I pray, "So, help me God!"

Fusing Horizons

Introduction

Just as it is important for the context within which a biblical text was produced to be considered for meaningful exegesis, so also the worldview of the readers a commentary on the text is meant for must be brought into account for meaningful application. While the truths of the epistles of John are universal, the writer of this commentary has kept (as also other writers in this series) the need to fuse the horizon of the meaning of the text to the original readers with the horizon of the readers of the commentary. For this commentary in particular, the writer has kept in mind the needs within the African context with special attention given to those students with curiosity to understand the passage on the basis of the Greek text. While some isolated comments of application have been made in several places in the course of explaining the text, we would like here to make some more extensive statements on how the horizon of the text and the horizon of readers of the commentary fuse together.

The focus of the epistles of John is how those born of God should live and what they should believe. The "how" has as its basis an eternal fellowship extended to the readers through John as the author, and is dictated by the nature of God as light. This is applied to love as special area—whether expressed in general (as in 1 and 2 John) or in matter of hospitality as in the case of 3 John. The "what" centers on the identity of Jesus, whom John states without ambiguity is the Christ.

One approach in answering the question whether the central message of the epistles of John has relevance to the African context is to reflect on the African traditional practices and beliefs. A second approach is to examine current events as those define the needs of the readers of this commentary. While not neglecting African traditional practices and beliefs (especially lamenting what is being lost) the focus here will be on the second approach. It is in observing what is going on now that the 21st-century reader may find answers to their questions in the Johannine epistles.

Africa is large (and also changing) and for that reason Kenya will be used as a representative of other regions. Current events will be limited to those that have been highlighted in some select newspapers, namely, Daily Nation, Standard, and Star. Observations are made from the events of August 2019. It is not possible to mention all the events of the time but those mentioned properly represent the general needs in the society.

Consideration of Current State of things

Beginning with the church, and then later looking at the society at large, one of the major stories covered in recent news concerned what the Standard newspaper of August 12, 2019 (p. 4) described as "two splinter groups nearly engage in a fistfight." At the center of the episode was the removal of 15 members from a church register. The Star newspaper of August 15, 2019 (p. 6) carried an interview with a member of the church who said that the 15 were victimized for "challenging the church leadership over graft and embezzlement of resources." Whatever the truth is on this matter, the church was turned more into a place of "shouting matches and fights than sermons" (Standard, p. 12). This fails the test of fellowship which John says includes believers, leaders, and even God (1 John 1:3). It also fails the test of love, for where there is fighting (even of words) there is the absence of love. Love draws people together but hate tears them apart. Arguing that this is an isolated incident in a united church in Kenya may not be right. In the Star newspaper of August 14, 2019 (p. 19) there is the story of a pastor (of another church) who is quoted as having, not long ago, told those ministering under his leadership, "I will kick you out of my ministry, whoever you are." These definitely are not words of a leader promoting the eternal fellowship John talks about in 1 John 1:3 and the love that he lays before his readers throughout his writings.

Someone may attempt to justify some of these incidents by quoting 1 John 2:19 (. . . *they were not of us*) or 2 John 10 (. . . *do not even greet them*).

These two passages, however, focus on belief rather than on relationships. The church in Kenya, and in Africa, needs to recapture what could be dying slowly in the areas of exercising brotherly love as we handle each other. Should the church also accommodate corruption or nepotism in any way, as the allegation of one of the incidents mentioned above has it, it would be failing in its duty as representing God who is light (1 John 1:5). The membership of the church is "those who have been born of God" (1 John 3:9) and all members should reflect the character of God.

Turning to society at large, a glimpse of the three newspapers seem to indicate a report of an act of violence, murder, defilement, corruption, and the like almost everyday. This may be normal in every society because the fall of Adam has affected us all, but Kenya is one of the countries where churches are overcrowded on Sundays and over 80% of the population would identify themselves as Christians, or at least people of the church. Star newspaper of August 21, 2019 reports a woman killing her lover (p. 6) and a man killing his brother by hitting him with a hammer (p. 10) over a food dispute. These types of murders for small things are surprisingly many. Daily Nation of August 6, 2019 (p. 22) reported "tragedy as man is killed in fight over local brew," and Star of August 8 of the same year (p. 26) has "Man kills brother . . . over avocado." In the local brew incident the victim is said to have drunk the killer's mug of traditional brew without his permission and the avocado incident may have been the climax of a dispute over land, but even here the manifestation of moral decay when it comes to the application of love is evident.

The murder of a man thrown out of a speeding bus is reported in the Standard newspaper of August 13, 2019 (p. 13); the Daily Nation of August 15, 2019 (p. 21) reports, "Shock as trader's throat slit open in public"; and the Star newspaper (August 15, 2019; p. 2) tells of the result for the victim having earlier refused the killer's request to play a video game without paying. Instantaneous anger and meditated actions both lack love when treating other peoples' lives so casually.

If this is the daily happenings in Kenya, and knowing that they represent many more which never get to be reported, John's message of love needs to be preached over and over again. Many lives have, and are being lost for matters that can be easily settled through a dialogue or by inviting a third party. This absence of love is also evidenced when the society at large takes the law into its hands and executes in mob justice an alleged offender without trial. In one of the incidents reported above for example, the Daily Nation of August 15, 2019 (p. 21) reports that the police had to shoot in the air to disperse the crowd which was "baying for the suspects' blood." John's message of love calls for a society in which all of us are treated with love, whether we are recipients of help or recipients of justice.

Incidents connected with lust of the flesh and of the eyes (1 John 2:16) or corruption are also numerous. Daily Nation of August 12, 2019 (p. 12) reported that in the past seven years, the Teachers Service Commission "has sacked 1,228 teachers who had sex with learners" (that is, with their pupils or students). The Star newspaper of August 13, 2019 (p. 23) carries a report of an elderly man of 66 having defiled a girl 6 years old. Young ones also feature in the Daily Nation of August 7, 2019 (p. 21), where it is reported, "Boy, 13, in defilement case to undergo counseling." According to what was reported he had defiled a girl of 11 years of age. Standard newspaper of August 12, 2019 (p. 6) reports, "State pays sh100m to ghost retirees." The list could go on.

As one reads these accounts and many others, one can get the impression that nothing good is happening in Kenya. That is not the case. For example, there is an account in the Star newspaper (August 12, 2019; p. 13) of a man who is said to be "committed to helping the less privileged in society in various ways, including seeing many through school to help them transform their lives." A summary of his activities is expressed in these words: "Over the years he has helped many young people break from the yoke of vicious cycle of poverty." A second example is found in the Daily Nation of August 8, 2019 (p. 2), where a a woman assisted another woman give birth in a taxi, before the mother could reach hospital. The assisting woman's attention was drawn by the taxi driver's shouting for help. The paper reports that she "immediately dropped her bag and took her lesso, which she used to cover the woman and assisted her to deliver the baby." The paper further reports, "Shortly, other women came in to cover the vehicle to make sure there was privacy for the woman." When asked of her relationship with the new mother, her reply was "I don't know the woman, but she smiled after she delivered the baby." These and many others who exercise love like them are not like Diotrephes of 3 John. They are giving others cause to smile, which is what love does. John's message is meant to multiply such persons, something badly needed in Kenya, in Africa, and the world.

While moral decay is more threatening in Kenya than false teaching, there is also the need for the church to be awake on the matter of wrong teachings. Daily Nation of August 12, 2019 (p. 19) has the article "Atheists demand public holiday for recognition." This is in reaction to the provision of public holidays to honor other faiths, especially Christianity and Islam. Their argument is that declaring February 17 as an atheist holiday would "end the inequity rooted in history." While belief in God is prevalent among many sons and daughters of Africa, modernization is bringing in challenges that Africa must be prepared to deal with in the area of belief.

Few Comments on Africa Traditional Beliefs and Practices

While the present generation, in many parts of Africa, does not care that much about their heritage in terms of beliefs and practices, some of the practices and beliefs are of so much relevance that we must seek ways of building on them. We must not lose them. Some of the ones we note in relation to the message of the epistles of John include:

1. The place of an elder (a title John uses for himself several times) in the African society. The title carried not only authority but also dependable truths of history. The focus was not that of an "office" but of a "function" rooted on having experienced issues of life for longer time. Modernization seems to be introducing an attitude where once the elderly have provide for, one can manage affairs of the church and society without consulting them. This fails to appreciate the fact that the elderly are a living library when it comes to life experiences in general.

2. The seriousness of sin (or taboo), which was viewed as the cause of lack of harmony in society, whether among the living or with the spiritual world. It is true we cannot address the matter the way it was addressed traditionally because we now know that it is only Jesus who is our *hilasmos* (1 John 2:2) and advocate (1 John 2:1) but the sensitivity that sin separates us from God (robbing us this wonderful fellowship) needs to be kept alive.

3. The need to exercise love to fellow members of the community. While this had the deficiency of limiting the community to fellow tribespeople, the concept can still be used as we promote love of God among all those who have been born of God. Our community, as believers, has no geographical, tribal, or racial limitations, and so love is to be given to whoever and wherever it is needed.

4. Hospitality. Someone who would act like the Diotrephes of 3 John would, in the African traditional setting, be an outcast. Whether there was little

or much, a visitor was counted among those with whom one would share what is available.

5. Deep sense of community or fellowship. A child, for example—in both matters of provision and also disciple—did not belong to a family but to the community. While this overlaps with number 3 above, it needs to be added here that this community included even those who had died within the last four or five generations, usually referred to as "the living dead." The good wish of the living dead was kept alive even as a new generation was nurtured.

Conclusion

In summary, Africa, which was once referred to as "dark continent," is deeply penetrated with the Gospel and is no dark continent in the context of exposure to western way of life, but there is much to do in making sure that the darkness of sin does not have a strong hold of the continent.

John's message in the epistles is not only relevant as we handle the ethical challenges of our day, but also as we strive to keep undiluted doctrines of our faith. This is important not only because we believe it is the infallible word of God, but also because what is taught in them has direct relationship to what our fathers and mothers in Africa traditionally practiced and believed. May the Lord help us as we strive to continually make sure the message of the epistles is not only understood but also relevantly applied to the African context. May the "African good" being lost find in us faithful custodians, and the evils attacking African society challenge us to be brave promoters of John's message of love and truth.

APPENDIX

Shade Terms used in this Work, Brief explanation

Verb Tenses

Present tense

1. Aoristic present – action that coincides with time of speaking or writing.

2. Durative/progressive present – action that began in the past and continuing at time of writing or speaking

3. Futuristic present – action that is yet to take place but is so certain that a present tense form is used to express it.

4. Gnomic present – action that usually takes place when the expected conditions are right.

5. Iterative present – action that occurs from time to time, with intervals.

6. Perfective present – action that focuses on the present reality of past action

Aorist tense

1. Constative aorist – an aorist verb that looks at the action as a whole, no matter how long it took.

2. Dramatic aorist – an aorist verb that expresses an action as having just happened.

3. Epistolary aorist – an aorist verb that captures an action

as happening during the time of the reader.

4. Gnomic aorist – an aorist expressing an action as happening like that all the time, as long as the conditions are right.

5. Inceptive aorist – an aorist focusing on the beginning of the action it expresses.

6. Resultative aorist – an aorist focusing on the conclusion of the action it expresses.

7. Proleptic aorist – an aorist expressing an action that is still future but is so certain that the writer views it as done.

Future tense

1. Predictive future – a verb in future tense whose focus is to affirm what will happen.

2. Volitive future – a verb in future tense, whose force is that of an imperative.

Perfect tense

1. Extensive perfect – a perfect verb form which focuses on the process or action, though not denying the result of the same.

2. Intensive perfect – a perfect verb form which focuses on the result, though not denying the process/action

Imperfect tense

Durative imperfect – an imperfect verb form that focuses on the progress of the action in the past.

Noun Cases

Genitive case

1. Epexegetical genitive – a noun in the genitive case whose function is to identify or define another noun more specifically.

2. Genitive of content – a noun in the genitive case that tells the reader what is contained in the noun it describes.

Appendix

3. Genitive of source or origin – a noun in genitive case whose function, in the context, is to tell the reader or hearer the origin of the noun it describes.

4. Genitive of association – a noun in genitive case, telling the reader or hearer with whom or with what another noun is associated with.

5. Objective genitive – a noun in the genitive case that tells the reader who or what the recipient of the action (implied) is.

6. Subjective genitive – a noun in the genitive case that tells the reader who or what the doer of the action (implied) is.

7. Qualitative genitive – a noun in the genitive case whose function is the quality of the noun it describes. Attributed genitive reverses the function. The noun in genitive is described rather than doing the describing.

Dative case

1. Dative of direct object – a noun in dative case serving as direct object.

2. Dative of sphere – a noun in dative case that spells out the sphere in which action takes place.

3. Dative of manner – a noun in dative case that tells the reader or hearer the manner in which an action takes place or it is done.

Accusative case

1. Accusative of reference – a noun in accusative case whose focus is to tell the reader with respect to what an action (implied) happens.

2. Accusative of termination – a noun in accusative case, used adverbially to tell the reader the goal or destination of an action.

3. Accusative of manner – a noun in accusative case whose focus is to spell out how an action is done.

Appendix

Moods

> Cohortative indicative – an indicative whose function, within its context, is to express a command.
>
> Declarative indicative – an indicative whose function is to make a statement.

Other

> Granville Sharp theory/rule. A summary statement of this is that if two substantives in the same case are joined by *kai* with an article found with the first and no article with the second, the two substantives refer to the same person.

Bibliography

Bauer, Walter. 1957. *A Greek-English Lexicon of the New Testament and other Early Christian Literature*. Translated by William F. Arndt and F. Wilbur Gingrich. Chicago: University of Chicago Press.

Baugh, S. M. 1999. *A First John Reader: Intermediate Greek Reading Notes and Grammar*. Phillipsburg: P & R.

Brooke, A. E. 1912. *A Critical and Exegetical Commentary on the Johannine Epistles*. 1976 Impression. Edinburgh: T. & T. Clark.

Brooks, James A., and Carlton L. Winbery. 1979. *Syntax of New Testament Greek*. Lanham, MD: United Press of America.

Brown, Raymond E. 1982. *The Epistles of John: Translated with Introduction, Notes and Commentary*. The Anchor Bible Series 30. Garden City, NY: Doubleday.

———. 1988. *The Gospel and Epistles of John: A Concise Commentary*. Collegeville, MN: Liturgical.

———. 1997. *An Introduction to New Testament*. New York: Doubleday.

Bruce, F. F. 1970. *The Epistles of John: Introduction, Exposition and Notes*. Grand Rapids: Eerdmans. Reprint 1983.

Burdick, Donald W. 1985. *The Letters of John the Apostle: An In-Depth Commentary*. Chicago: Moody.

Burge, Gary M. 1996. *The Letters of John*. The NIV Application Commentary. Grand Rapids: Zondervan.

Burton, Ernest De Witt. 1978. *Syntax of the Moods and Tenses in New Testament Greek*. Grand Rapids: Kregel.

Culy, Martin M. 2004. *I, II, III John: A Handbook on the Greek Text*. Waco, TX: Baylor University Press.

Carson, D. A. 1991. *The Gospel According to John*. Grand Rapids: Eerdmans.

Carson, D. A., and Douglas J. Moo. 2005. *An Introduction to the New Testament*. 2nd ed. Grand Rapids: Zondervan.

Cruse, C. F. 1894. *The Ecclesiastical History of Eusebius Pamphilus. Translated from the Greek*. London: George Bell & Sons.

Dana, H. E., and Julius R. Mantey. 1957. *A Manual Grammar of the Greek New Testament*. Toronto: Macmillan.

deSilva, David S. 2004. *An Introduction to the New Testament Context, Methods and Ministry Formation*. Downers Grove, IL: Intervarsity.

Doty, William G. 1973. *Letters in Primitive Christianity*. Philadelphia: Fortress.

Bibliography

Finegan, Jack. 1974. *Encountering New Testament Manuscripts: A Working Introduction to Textual Criticism*. Grand Rapids: William B. Eerdmans.

Fitzgerald, J. T. 2000. "Hospitality." In *Dictionary of New Testament Background*, edited by Craig E. Evans et al., 522–25. Downers Grove, IL: Inter-Varsity.

Gingrich, F. Wilbur. 1965. *Shorter Lexicon of the Greek New Testament*. Chicago: The University of Chicago Press.

Gorder, Paul R. Van. 1978. *In the Family: Studies in First John*. Grand Rapids: Radio Bible Class.

Guthrie, Donald. 1970. *New Testament Introduction*. Downers Grove, IL: Inter-Varsity.

Grayston, Kenneth. 1984. *The Johannine Epistles*. The New Century Bible Commentary. Grand Rapids: Eerdmans.

Griffith, Terry. 2002. *Keep Yourselves from Idols: A New Look at 1 John*. London: Sheffield.

Haas, C., et al. 1972. *A Translator's Handbook on the Letters of John*. London: United Bible Societies.

Harrison, Everett F. 1971. *Introduction to the New Testament*. Rev. ed. Grand Rapids: Eerdmans.

Hauck, Friedrich. 1965. "κοινός, κοινωνός, κοινωνέω, κοινωνία, συγκοινωνός, συγκοινωνέω, κοινωνικός, κοινόω." In vol. 3 of *TDNT*, edited by Gerhard Kittel, 789–809. Translated by Geoffrey W. Bromiley. Grand Rapids: Eerdmans.

Hobbs, Herschel H. 1983. *The Epistles of John*. Nashville: Thomas Nelson.

Houlden, J. L. 1973. *The Johannine Epistles*. Harper's New Testament Commentaries. New York: Harper & Row.

Jackman, David. 1988. *The Message of John's Letters*. The Bible Speaks Today. Downers Grove, IL: Inter-Varsity.

Jobes, Karen H. 2014. *1, 2 & 3 John*. Exegetical Commentary on New Testament. Grand Rapids: Zondervan.

Keener, Craig S. 1993. *The IVP Bible Background Commentary: New Testament*. Downers Grove, IL: Inter-Varsity.

———. 2003. *The Gospel of John*. Vol. 1. Peabody, MA: Hendrickson.

Kruse Colin G. 2000. *The Letters of John*. Grand Rapids: Eerdmans.

Kysar, Robert. 1986. *I, II, III John*. Augsburg Commentary on the New Testament. Minneapolis: Augsburg.

Kistemaker, Simon J. 1986. *James and I–III John*. New Testament Commentary Series. Grand Rapids: Baker.

Kummel, Werner Georg. 1975. *Introduction to the New Testament*. Nashville: Abingdon.

Lieu, Judith M. 1991. *Theology of the Johannine Epistles*. Cambridge: Cambridge University Press.

———. 2008. *I, II & III John: A Commentary*. Louisville: Westminster John Knox.

Marshall, I. Howard. 1978. *The Epistles of John*. The New International Commentary on the New Testament. Grand Rapids: Eerdmans.

Martinez, Florentino Garcia. 1994. *The Dead Sea Scrolls Translated: The Qumran Text in English*. Leiden: E. J. Brill.

Mati, J. K. G. 2014. *Healers to Physicians: Memories of a Divergent Past—A Personal Story*. Nairobi: IRHTR Occasional Publications.

Moulton, James Hope. 1963. *A Grammar of New Testament Greek*. Vol. 3, *Syntax*. Edinburgh: T. & T. Clark.

Bibliography

Moulton James Hope, and George Milligan. 1930. *The Vocabulary of the Greek Testament: Illustrated from the Papyri and Other Non-Literary Sources*. Grand Rapids: Eerdmans. Reprint 1982.

Ngewa, Samuel M. 2003. *The Gospel of John for Pastors and Teachers*. Nairobi: Evangel.

―――. 2009. *1 & 2 Timothy and Titus*. Africa Bible Commentary Series. Grand Rapids: Zondervan.

Oepke, Albrecht. 1967. "παῖς, παιδίον, παιδάριον, τέκνον, τεκνίον, βρέφος." In vol. 5 of *TDNT*, edited by Gerhard Kittel, 635–54. Translated by Geoffrey W. Bromiley. Grand Rapids: Eerdmans.

Painter, John. 2003. *1, 2 and 3 John*. Sacra Pagina Series 18. Collegeville, MN: Liturgical.

Plummer, Alfred. 1888. *The Epistles of St. John*. Thornapple Commentaries. Grand Rapids: Baker. Reprint 1980.

Schattenmann, Johannes. 1975. "Fellowship, Have, Share, Participate." In vol. 1 of *DNTT*, edited by Colin Brown, 635–44. Grand Rapids: Zondervan.

Schnackenburg, Rudolf. 1992. *The Johannine Epistles: Introduction and Commentary*. Translated by Reginald and Ilse Fuller. New York: Crossroad.

Smalley, Stephen S. 1984. *1, 2, 3 John*. Word Biblical Commentary 51. Waco, TX: Word Books.

Stott, John. 1964. *The Epistles of John: An Introduction and Commentary*. The Tyndale New Testament Commentaries. Grand Rapids: Eerdmans.

Thomas, John Christopher. 2004. *The Pentecostal Commentary on 1 John, 2 John, 3 John*. London: T & T. Clark.

Wallace, Daniel B. 1996. *Greek Grammar Beyond the Basics: An Exegetical Syntax of the New Testament*. Grand Rapids: Zondervan.

Westcott, Brooke Foss. 1892. *The Epistles of St. John: The Greek Text, with Notes and Addenda*. Grand Rapids: Eerdmans.

Wise, Michael O., et al. 2005. *The Dead Sea Scrolls*. San Francisco: Harper Collins.

Yarbrough, Robert W. 2008. *1–3 John*. Grand Rapids: Baker Academic.

Scripture Index

(passages outside the letters of John)

Genesis

1:1	14, 48
1:4	20n47
1:10	20n47
1:12	20n47
1:18	20n47
1:21	20n47
1:25	20n47
1:31	20n47
3:6, 17	42
3:8–10	54n146
3:12–13	20
3:17–18	20

Leviticus

19:18	31n74, 103n30

Numbers

18:22	92n295
12:8	110n62

Deuteronomy

17:6	12, 88
19:15	12
22:20–25	92

1 Samuel

13:14	28

2 Samuel

11	28

Psalms

14:2–3	24
51:5	24
130:3	24
143:2	24

Isaiah

6:1	124
6:5	23
22:14	92
61:8	73

Matthew

3:17	31n73, 87n274
3:13–17	87
4:9	42
4:1–11	38, 41
5:23–24	77
5:43–48	34
5:44	83
6:7	91
6:24	40
7:7	90
12:31	91n290
12:50	126
13:55–56	81n251

Scripture Index

Matthew (*continued*)

14:55, 56, 59	10n6
16:16–18	44n144
16:18	126
17:1–8	2n7
18:16	12n15
20:28	33n81
22:37	76
23:31	10n3
24:4–5, 11, 14	46n120
26:37–46	3n7
27:32–56	87
28:19–20	11n9

Mark

1:9–11	87
1:11	87n274
3:28–30	91n290
3:32	81n251
5:37–42	2n7
9:2–19	2n7
10:45	33n81, 107n50
12:30	76
13:22	46n120
14:33–42	3n7
15:21–41	87

Luke

3:21–22	87
3:22	87n274
4:1–13	38, 41
4:6	42, 42n108
4:22	10n3
8:51–56	2n7
9:28–36	2n7
10:27	76
12:10	91n290
22:15	41n105
22:71	10n6
23:26–49	87

John

1:1	2n6, 14n23, 15
1:10	40n103
1:11	53
1:12	50n136
1:14	2n6, 14n23, 15n28, 51n141, 70
1:29	40n103
3:3, 4, 5, 6, 7	2n6
3:16	72n224, 106n43
9:5	32
10:11	30
13:23–24	3n7
13:33	36
13:34	2n6
13:34–35	31n74
14:6	16, 68n199, 100n18
14:7–11	38
14:16	2n6, 26n56
14:26	47n126, 48n131
15:12	32n77
15:13	30, 32
15:26	2n6
16:7	2n6
16:33	70, 81n250
19:16–37	87
20:2	3n7
20:31	5, 81, 89
21:24	2

Acts

4:12	81n249
7:56	51n142
8:32	56n150
12:2	3n7
13:22	28
14:26–27	118n54
17:11	67n192
19:20	116n43
20:28	87
22:18	10n6
23:30	39n99

Romans

3:10–18	24
5:12	20
5:19	42
8:19–21	20n47
8:21	10n4
8:35–39	89

Scripture Index

8:36	56n150
10:2	10n4
16:23	116n43

1 Corinthians

1:14	116n43
3:10–15	106n44
11:30	93
15:15	10n4

2 Corinthians

8:3	10n4
13:1	12n15

Galatians

2:11	63n172
2:20	72n224
4:15	10n4
6:11	39n99

Ephesians

2:20	44n114
5:32	78n243
6:17	38
6:22	39n99

Philippians

2:28	39n99
3:7	42

Colossians

1:15	46
1:20	87
1:15–20	46n119
3:1	51n142
4:8	39n99
4:13	10n4

1 Thessalonians

2:17	41n105

2 Thessalonians

2:3	46n120, 68n196

1 Timothy

3:7	10n6
5:10	10n4
5:19	12n15
6:13	10n4

2 Timothy

3:1	46n122

Titus

1:13	10n6

Philemon

12	39n99

Hebrews

1:2	46n122
1:3	51n142
13:12	87

James

4:2	90
5:3	46n122
5:5	56n150

1 Peter

1:15	73n228
1:19	26n58, 87
1:20	46n122
2:22	26n58
4:8	33
5:9	57

2 Peter

3:3	46n122

Revelation

1:2	10n5
2:6	73
5:6, 12	56n150
6:9	10n6, 56n150
11:7	10n6
12:11, 17	10n6
13:8	56n150

Revelation (*continued*)

18:24	56n150
19:10	10n6
20:4	10n6
20:10	58
21:9	77n239
21:22–27	33
22:16, 18, 20	10n5
22:21	48

Author Index

Bauer, Walter, 36n89, 135
Baugh, S. M., 52n143, 61n167, 65n182, 135
Brooke, A. E., 2n6, 13n21, 35n86, 65n181, 70n207, 73n229, 75n234, 78n242, 87n272, 89n279, 91n290, 135
Brooks J. A., 13n19, 135
Brown, R. E., 4n13, 5n14, 12n13, 13n19, 14n24, 35, 35n86, 35n87, 51n140, 87n272, 89n278, 105n37, 135
Bruce, F. F., 34n84, 70n205, 89n280, 92n295, 135
Burdick, D. W., 12n13, 13, 13n18, 13n21, 35n86, 51n140, 70n205, 89n280, 135
Burge, G. M., 51n140, 52n143, 70n205, 82n256, 92n295, 100n21, 101n22, 109n55, 121n56, 135
Carson, D. A., 3n9, 80n247, 135
Culy, M. M., 8, 8n26, 51n140, 61n167, 100n21, 102n26, 121n56, 135
Dana H. E and Mantey J. R, 13n19, 135
deSilva, D. S., 4n13, 7n22, 135
Doty, William G., 1n3, 135
Finegan, Jack, 8n23, 136
Fitzgerald J. T., 122n57, 136
Gingrich, F. W., 106n46, 111n9, 117n52, 136
Gorder, P. R. Van, 34n84, 136
Guthrie, Donald, 2n4, 3n11, 136

Grayston, Kenneth, 51n140, 52n143, 63n173, 89n278, 91n290, 136
Griffith, Terry, 96n300, 136
Haas C., 34n83, 37n94, 89n278, 136
Hauck, Friedrich, 16n36, 136
Hobbs, H. H., 51n140, 52n143, 62n169, 64n176, 81n252, 82n257, 91n290, 100n18, 100n21, 106n42, 107n51, 136
Houlden, J. L., 51n140, 82n256, 136
Jackman, D., 88n278, 91n290, 136
Jobes, Karen H., 2n6, 3n8, 5n16, 7, 7n21, 12n13, 14, 14n25, 36, 36n91, 44n111, 46n122, 47n126, 52n143, 67n189, 68n200, 77, 77n238, 82n259, 91n290, 100n18, 100n21, 106n43, 136
Keener, C. S., 3n7, 3n9, 80n247, 136
Kruse C. G., 15n26, 28n66, 34n83, 35n86, 35n88, 40, 40n100, 40n102, 46n120, 47n126, 51n140, 52n143, 62n169, 63n172, 63n173, 69n201, 70n205, 79, 79n246, 82n257, 91n290, 92n295, 100n18, 100n21, 101n24, 102n26, 103n32, 105n37, 105n41, 106n43, 136
Kysar, Robert, 51n140, 52n143, 62n169, 70n207, 82n257, 91n290, 100n18, 100n21, 102n26, 107n51, 109n55, 136

Author Index

Kistemaker, S. J. ,16n34, 35n86, 70n206, 89n278, 91n290, 92n295, 136
Kummel, W. G., 8n24, 136
Lieu, J. M., 6, 6n18, 6n19, 10, 10n7, 15n26, 28n64, 35n85, 36, 36n92, 44n113, 47n126, 51n140, 62n169, 82n256, 87n272, 106n42, 107n51, 109n55, 110n63, 136
Marshall, I. H., 37n94, 87n270, 104n33
Mati, J. K. G., xiii, 136
Moulton J. H., 13n19, 36, 36n89, 36n90, 136
Ngewa, S. M., 1n1, 3n7, 5n15, 11n12, 46n122, 137
Oepke, Albrecht, 36n89, 137
Painter, John, 2n4, 2n6, 51n140, 52n143, 61n166, 62n169, 64n179, 70n207, 82n257, 87n273, 91n290, 92n295, 100n21, 102n26, 102n29, 107n51, 137
Plummer, Alfred, 11n12, 13n18, 14n24, 34n83, 51n140, 52n143, 92n295, 137
Schattenmann, J., 16n36, 137

Schnackenburg, R., 3n11, 17, 18n40, 28n65, 35n86, 51n140, 65, 65n180, 68n200, 92n295, 100n18, 107n51, 137
Smalley, S. S., 8n25, 12n13, 13n20, 14n22, 16n35, 35n86, 37n94, 38n97, 51n140, 87n272, 137
Stott, John, 10, 10n8, 13, 13n18, 13n21, 34n84, 52n143, 70n205, 105n37, 137
Thomas, J. C., 62n170, 65n182, 66n184, 67n189, 68n200, 72, 72n222, 81n253, 82n257, 92n295, 100n18, 100n21, 101n22, 105n37, 106n43, 107n51, 137
Wallace, D. B., 13n19, 40n102, 41n107, 57n152
Westcott, B. F., 13n18, 16n34, 35n86, 51n140, 52n143, 137
Yarbrough, R. W., 3n11, 5, 5n17, 25n55, 26, 26n59, 27, 27n59, 27n61, 27n62, 28n66, 51n140, 52n143, 69n201, 70n206, 72n223, 82n257, 87n273, 91n290, 100n21, 102n26, 102n29, 104, 104n34, 106n43, 107n46, 137

Subject Index

Agapē, philia, storgē, eros (love), 33n81
Agapētoi (beloved), 31n73, 75n233
Apangellein (to announce), 10
Antichristos (antichrist), 44n116, 68n195
Chrisma (anointing), 47n126
Docetism, 44n112
Ebionism, 44n112
Eidōlon, (idol) 96
Eschate hōra (last hour), 46n122
Hilasmos (propitiation, expiation) 27
Jehovah's witnesses, 45, 45n118, 46n119, 107n49
Koinōnia (fellowship), 16n36
Kosmos (world), 40n103
Logos (word), 2n6, 38n96
Martyrein/martyria (witness), 10
Oida and ginōsko (I know), 28n63, 37n93, 95
Paracletos (advocate), 2n6, 26n56
Parresia (confidence), 54n147
Phōs (light), 19, 19n46
Presbyteros (elder), 99n16
Prōtotokos (firstborn), 46n119
Skandalon (snare, stumbling block), 33n82
Skotia (darkness), 19n46
Splanchna (bowels of mercy), 60n162

Greek Concepts Index

Accusative case
    of reference, 23n52, 133
    of manner, 115n41, 133
    of termination, 59n157, 86n271, 112n12, 133
Aorist tense
    Constative, 29n70, 86n270, 97n302, 99n15, 111n4, 116n46, 131
    Dramatic, 98n7, 131
    Epistolary, 30n71, 39, 43n110, 88n275, 99n15, 131
    Gnomic, 80n248, 132
    Inceptive, 86n270, 132
    Proleptic, 19n43, 19n44, 48n132, 113n20, 132
    Resultative, 13, 30n71, 32n80, 49n134, 70n209, 112n14, 132
Cohortative indicative 72n221, 82n260, 134
Dative case
    of direct object, 23n52, 66n185, 85n268, 133
    of manner, 100n18, 114n30, 133
    of means 12, 102n26, 114n30
    of possession, 23n52
    of respect/reference, 71n210, 111n6, 112n17, 114n36
    of sphere, 98n3, 100n18, 101n22, 102n26, 111n1, 133
Declarative indicative, 82n255, 134
Durative imperfect, 15n29, 98n8, 132
Future tense
    Predictive, 67n190, 92n292, 98n4, 101n23, 101n24, 113n28, 132

    Progressive, 112n18
    Volitive, 88n277, 92n292, 132
Genitive case
    Attributed, 133
    Epexegetical, 64n178, 101n25, 132
    Objective, 16n31, 28, 29n68, 41, 60n163, 69n204, 83, 107n51, 133
    of association, 98n5, 133
    of content, 107, 132
    of direct object, 61n168, 90n286
    of exit, 59n156
    of relationship, 49n135, 50n137, 89n282
    of source or origin, 38, 47n128, 51n140, 68n197, 133
    of the whole, 102n27, 113n25
    Qualitative, 28, 29n67, 29n68, 51n140, 60, 68n197, 89n281, 133
    Subjective, 28, 29n68, 38, 50n139, 107n51, 113n29, 133
Granville Sharp theory/rule, 106n45, 134
Perfect tense
    Extensive, 13n17, 18n41, 105n37, 132
    Intensive, 13n17, 18n41, 37, 37n95, 59n155, 59n159, 66n187, 71n211, 71n212, 76n236, 98n2, 100n19, 102n29, 105n37, 114n35, 132

Greek Concepts Index

Present tense
    Aoristic, 11n10, 102n28, 109n60,
        111n7, 114n38, 115n39, 131
    Durative, 11n10, 32n79, 38, 52,
        53n144, 64n176, 95n298,
        95n299, 102n28, 103n31,
        107n47, 111n3, 111n7,
        116n47, 131
    Dramatic, 105n37
    Futuristic, 46n120, 64n175,
        90n288, 131
    Gnomic/Customary, 19n45,
        50n138, 53n144, 62n171,
        63n174, 90n285, 107n48, 108,
        124n62, 131
    Iterative, 11n10, 21, 22, 45n117,
        67n192, 90n283, 109n60,
        113n23, 114n33, 117n50,
        121, 131
    Perfective, 22n50, 38, 105n37,
        107n47, 131
    Tendential, 45n117, 85
Prohibition, 40n102, 57n152, 66n184,
    108n54, 124n60

www.ingramcontent.com/pod-product-compliance
Lightning Source LLC
Chambersburg PA
CBHW030859170426
43193CB00009BA/667